Foolish Wisdom

Stories, Activities, and Reflections from Ken Feit, I.F. (Itinerant Fool)

Joseph F. Martin, F.I.C.

Resource Publications, Inc.
San Jose, California

Editorial Director: Kenneth Guentert
Production Editor: Kathi Drolet
Art Director: Terri Ysseldyke-All

Photo Credits:
Cover and page 15: Courtesy *Creation*
Page 39: Courtesy Henri Nouwen

Reprint Department
Resource Publications, Inc.
160 E. Virginia Street, Suite 290
San Jose, CA 95112-5848

Library of Congress Cataloging in Publication Data

Martin, Joseph F., 1944–
    Foolish Wisdom : stories, activities , and reflections
from Ken Feit, I.F. / Joseph F. Martin.
        p.   cm.
    Includes bibliographic references.
    ISBN 0-89390-174-1
    1. Meditations. 2. Feit, Ken, 1940–1981.
3. Clowns—Religious aspects—Christianity. 4. Activity
programs in Christian education.
I. Title.
BX2182.2.M335 1990
282. 092—dc20

5 4 3 2 1

94 93 92 91 90

Dedication

To Mom and Dad
Joseph W. Martin
Genevieve T. Schultz

To the memory of Benjamin Linder
engineer, clown, juggler, unicyclist, visionary
murdered by U.S. backed Contras
April 28, 1987
in San Jose de Bocay, Nicaragua

a United States worker
killed by those who espouse United States ideals
using arms paid for by United States taxpayers

"Podran matar las flores pero no la primavera."
(They can kill the flowers but they can't kill spring.)

Contents

Foreword

It was the mid-seventies and of course I was staying in a commune that offered workshops on the full-time gamut of new-age-ness. I was developing my interest in clowning which was a way that our socially conscious generation was catching its breath in the midst of Vietnam, Watergate, and the like. Occasionally, I heard the name "Ken Feit" drift through conversations, usually surrounded by a context of what sounded to me like political-psycho-babble. Everyone's looking for a guru, I thought to myself, but I listened because it sounded like here was not your average hippy-philosopher fool.

The Association of Humanistic Psychology held a summer conference on the Princeton campus. The first day's event was a parade that stood still while the people walked by. Mimes, magicians, puppeteers, belly dancers, storytellers, fiddlers on roofs, fantasy characters from Greek mythology, Don Quixote fighting an "X"-shaped sculpture, etc. All were scattered in their places throughout the landscaping and architecture of the campus while three thousand conference participants strolled by in groups of a hundred. I was eating fire, quite heatedly, for three hours in a Gothic stone archway. Afterward, I heard stories that at the parade's end there was some strange character sitting over in a dumpster telling haiku poems. People weren't quite sure whether he was supposed to be there officially or not. But some decided to go over and listen. Nobody knew his name.

The next day my roommate told me that she had just been to a three-hour unscheduled performance of life-shaking depth and playfulness by a man named Ken Feit. I was dressed in an outrageous clown costume in preparation for a rowdy evening Mardi Gras event. Carrying my fire-eating equipment, I ran across the campus and up the steps to the building she had named. Out of breath, I crashed right into a man as he exited the door. "Do you know where Ken Feit is staying?" I asked. "I'm Ken Feit." he replied. We had a rushed conversation of introductions, schedules, and a decision of when I might get to study with him, and I ran off to my appointed show time. He, being tired from the performance, was going to sleep. (Five years later, he told me that he changed his mind and came to the explosive party to observe quietly who this crazy woman was.) The previous day's parade venue was to perform on two continuous stages, but in the rowdy evening energy only a small handful of acts could handle the crowd: the Dixieland band, the belly dancer, and my partner and myself, who ate fire and just played with the audience.

As a beginning clown, my material was lousy, my confidence was low, but my heart was enthusiastic. When I began an apprenticeship with him that lasted until and beyond his death, it was my flame of enthusiasm which he fanned for me and continues to fan. We didn't go over my material or work on stories appropriate for my telling. We stayed in touch and crossed paths whenever we could, spending weeks together between and during various engagements in North America and Europe. When we came toward each other in airports or bus stations he would hold his ears because he hated jokes, and so I loved to tell them to him. He wanted "real stories, not trumped up ones." Yet he's the one who would preface himself with, "Some stories, if they aren't true, ought to be true, so therefore ..."

Ken had a powerful and charismatic presence. He was over six feet tall, with long and lanky arms and legs, a boyish grin, a warm and easy laugh, mixed with a scholar's cool intensity. He told me that he knew that he was fluid and graceful with his upper body in performance, but he felt klutzy in his lower body, which is why he sat cross-legged on the floor to tell stories, enchanting everyone for three full hours using only his head and arms and minimal props. Always one to dare himself and others into incongruous playfulness, it was only in the month before his death that he was able to bring himself to disco dance at a bar with a group of friends, and then only because he could relate it to African tribal rhythms. But he felt silly—this man who could harmonica and soap bubble his way down the streets of Paris.

Ken insisted that he was but a flute through which his stories came. His preparation time before performance was a ritual of silent, shamanistic centering. At the same time he was the consummate entertainer (a word he hated) in the sense that he was deft at the contracts, honoraria, and other politics of his trade. When he and his students both could grow past putting him on a pedestal as teacher, then he became a mentor in the art of bringing folly into this world and surviving at the same time. He especially helped women by encouraging them to claim their economic worth as teachers and performers.

As I entered the theatre in the place where I was to attend a workshop and see one of his performances, I stumbled a little in the dark aisle and hesitantly climbed the side stairs onto the stage. Some large table lamps had been brought from somebody's living room and placed in front of a carpet piece where sat a large and lanky man with crossed legs and closed eyes. The audience gathered in a half-circle on the stage boards and listened to the tape playing strange and eerie chants and rhythms from other worlds than we knew. I thought nervously, "This is too California for me."

Ken Feit opened his eyes, swept us with a welcoming smile, changed the tape to the classical lightness of Vivaldi's *Four Seasons*, took a brown paper lunch bag, and began to explore the objects therein. How could such simple stories be so endearing? Thank heaven it was not the mawkish pointing-to-itself style of clowning that tries so hard to be child-like but comes off childish. But simple objects became simple stories. Some make-up, a banana and a needle and thread, a popcorn kernel and a spoonful of oil, matches and paper and scissors—a wordless hour passed by.

Ken looked at a card with a "W" squiggle on it. "Wough" he uttered (as in the first part of "woof")—the first sound to surprise the silence. "Wough" again and different in curious explorations until he dropped the card, and it turned upside down. "Mmmm," he mused. And now "M" became sounds and ears and moos and it dropped. Fingers held over a section brought out an "I," then an "S," then an "E" —sounds became letters and single letters became words and words together became sentences all from fingers playing around one squiggle. And we laughed and Ken eased into talking.

Flowing scarves told a story of the battle of the seasons. Sounds from a glass of water, a straw, and a balloon full of beans told a frog story. White make-up and a kimono, which flowed onto his person even as he was still cross-legged on the floor, led into haikus with hand poetry, sometimes illuminated in shadow pictures on the wall cast by a single candle. The white make-up came off, and on came dark make-up and his rag-scarf became a turban for Akhi, the beggar. The make-up wiped off, now a peasant headscarf, two rolled up socks and the padding of his other shirt made him a pregnant Appalachian woman fretting over the pregnancy of her child, America. A different make-up, and American Indian creation stories were told with punctuation by feathers as choreography.

Ken wrote or recreated all of his stories. He told me once that he knew five thousand stories. I was entranced by his depth of knowledge and memory and I asked him, "How do you do it? What's your discipline? Do you spend so many hours a day in certain study, exercises, or practice?" He answered, "No, I'm just a dumb shit. I just keep myself in work because when a job's coming up, you *have* to do something toward it." Having just spent several years with some very driven performers of various schools I thought, "Ah, the teacher for me."

Ken was as humble as he was proud. He easily encouraged and networked artists that he met. And he surrounded himself at workshops with women who had come with an understanding that they were especially invited, then left it for them to work things out among themselves. He espoused and modeled the life of an itinerant wed to poverty, while he was also known to leave international phone bills behind him. He was exceedingly generous with his money, lending to and supporting many friends in quiet ways. And he was able to command contracts as a skilled professional, speaking fluently the language of the "white, male, adult world." After his death, a friend teased me, "How is the beatification process going for St. Ken?" We laughed because it was at once painfully true and ludicrous.

On his annual trek around another continent, he would enter the consulate and perform for the ambassadors, who would then call ahead to the universities and say, "I can't tell you what this guy does, but hire him!" When he visited Mother Teresa of Calcutta, he humbled himself in the presence of such pain, but she gently encouraged him to perform for the workers and share his own gifts in his own way.

One evening in San Francisco's Chinatown, the audience was quiet and stoic. When he came to the Oriental stories, he felt afraid that perhaps he was not worthy to perform them. He heard an elderly couple whisper their approval when he unfolded and folded the Japanese ceremonial robe in the correct manner; the audience then went with him. He was meticulously careful about all of his cultural and historical details. In a similar manner, the truth he invested in his character of Cleo, the Appalachian woman, had some of his friends calling him Sister Cleo. I myself would write letters to either Ken or Cleo as needed in discussions about relationships and perspectives.

In his early work in the streets of St. Louis, he was stopped one dark night by would-be attackers. In his fear he inadvertently popped out his partial plate, which he could maneuver like a bureau drawer. "Do that again!" they exclaimed, and the event ended with handshakes and some lasting friendships.

He rarely attended movies, preferring the energy of live theatre. But one night he decided to go see the new hit "Jaws." He had heard about the graphic scenes of violence to assorted humans, and as he was looking for a pleasant evening, he decided to go and see it through the eyes of a different species—a chicken. Before he bought his ticket, he walked around the block convincing himself that he was a chicken in a chicken's world. He then could sit through the rough scenes unperturbed, until disaster struck, and the cast sat down to a fried chicken dinner! His anguished response was the only one in the theatre.

When I received the phone message that somebody had died, I tried to prepare myself and imagine which friend in common it might be. When I returned the call and heard that it was Ken, I was shocked both by the news and by my response; I was thinking of everyone but him. Somehow he tickled the immortal edges. But that last summer he had been deeply tired. He was contemplating many major changes: perhaps in career, location, marital status. He was leaving a full week-long workshop in Berkeley and driving cross-country to prepare for leaving the country again.

Early morning brought the driving accident, the long wait for help in the Utah stretches, and the long drive to the nearest town. He asked his traveling companion, "Be quiet, please; I'm dying," and he stayed with that final journey until moments before arriving at the hospital.

Memorial services were held by friends throughout the United States, in London, Paris, Australia, and perhaps other places. This man was missed internationally because of his own powerful gifts of mind and heart as well as for his readiness to see and say "yes" to the powerful gifts in others.

In our early times together, we attended a party that followed his performance. It was wonderful, and we were teasing him because he knew it had been wonderful. I began to perform a playful parody of his performance, rewriting the stories: "When my house burned down, then I could get a better view ... of the woman next door taking a bath." He watched with glee, and said, "Every fool needs his clown." And every clown needs her fool.

The inter-cultural, traditional comic pair of the pompous and the buffoon is based on the interplay of fool and clown. Conrad Hyers writes that Chaplin was so famous because he had the rare ability of encompassing both at once in his costume and character. Ken did so in his own way, as he was able to be profound and playful, powerful and present. This book shows us some soap bubbles drifting by as Joe Martin could gently catch them. Some glisten with philosophy, and others shimmer with simplicity. Here are some rememberings and some gleanings from many resources. May you find some bubbles to catch your eye, some affirmation to catch your heart, some challenge to catch your mind, and some purely play to catch your breath.

As Ken would close,
Gently,

Margie Brown
Summer 1989

Acknowledgements

Many people have helped in significant ways with the writing and publishing of this book. I owe special gratitude to Helen Feit, Carol Weimer, Matthew Fox O.P., Margie Brown, Tria Thompson, David and Elisabeth Linder, Kenneth Guentert and Kathi Drolet.

Others made a special effort to help me—Adriana Diaz, Rose Eleanor Ehret S.N.J.M., Michael Sparough S.J., Floyd Shaffer, Ed Stivender, and Anne Marie Weiler.

Many teachers helped me develop my own clown/fool— Bill Peckham, Tom Woodward, Tom Sparough, Doug Adams, Tim Kehl, Megan McKenna, Jacquie (Walker) Mishoe, Leo Remington, Bill Pindar, David Parker, Joe Zsigray, Michael Moynahan S.J., Reid Gilbert, Leonard Auclair, Al Alter, Brian Goede—and many others from the Phoenix Power and Light Company.

Some offered suggestions or inspiration—Ray Jason, Robin Goodfellow, John Towsen, Nick Weber S.J., Lorenzo Pickle, Avner (the Eccentric) Eisenberg, Stanley Allen Sherman, Marcel Marceau, The Atomic Comics, Leonard Pitt, and The Flying Karamazov Brothers.

And speaking of brothers—special thanks to the Brothers of Christian Instruction who provided me a sabbatical year to complete research for this project.

Grateful acknowledgment is made to the following for permission to quote extensively from copyrighted materials:

Soundways: A Book of Sound Poems. Kenneth Feit. © 1971 by Loyola University Press, Chicago, IL. Used with permission.

"Creative Ministry." Ken Feit, I.F. © 1974 by *Celebration*, P.O. Box 281, Kansas City, MO, 64141. Used with permission.

"Laughter is a Sacrament." Ken Feit. © 1975 by *One World*, World Council of Churches, P.O. Box 66, 1211 Geneva 20, Switzerland. Used with permission.

"The Priestly Fool." Ken Feit. © 1975 by *Anglican Theological Review*, 600 Haven St., Evanston, IL, 60201. Used with permission.

"In Praise of Hands" and "Reflections of a Sound Poet." Ken Feit. © 1976 by The Liturgical Conference, 806 Rhode Island Ave. N.E., Washington, D.C., 20018. All rights reserved. Used with permission.

Fools for Christ. © 1982 by Cathedral Films, P.O. Box 4029, Westlake Village, CA, 91359. Used with permission.

Joseph F. Martin, F.I.C.

Introduction

When he lived in Milwaukee, Ken Feit had a business card printed that read "Ken, the fool—clown, sound poet, storyteller, puppeteer, mime, musician, and jester." He was a clown/fool, but he was no fool. While he was not a priest, he performed priestly functions. As an accomplished storyteller, he used the crafts of puppetry, mime, and music to enhance his stories.

Unlike clowns who simply show off their foolishness, Ken reflected deeply on the meanings of his performance skills and shared many insights with his audiences. After blowing bubbles one night in a Buddhist monastery in Burma, he reflected that

> one of the wonders of life is a bubble. It is born from human breath like a story. There's so much color alive inside each bubble. Each one is a window, a magic magnifying glass. No two bubbles are alike. Some spin while others are still. Some linger and have babies before your eyes, while others crash madly against walls and sidewalks. A bubble's life may seem short, but it never really dies. Like music or incense, a bubble blends with the rest of the world (KFS, 47).*

Ken Feit has blended with the rest of the world. Besides being a clown, mime, storyteller, puppeteer, musician, and jester, he saw himself also as a priest because he

*References to sources have three-letter codes that correspond to references in the bibliography. Numbers refer to pages.

gathered people and led celebrations. To these may be added two other roles—prophet and mystic, in the tradition of creation-centered spirituality. Although he had extraordinary talents and imagination, he was an ordinary human being. In his own words, "As Popeye and Yahweh say 'I am what I am and that's all that I am'" (KFB, 30).

On October 13, 1940, Ken was born in Chicago to a family of German background. Clarence and Helen Feit raised their children in a typical working-class neighborhood. Young Ken attended St. Cornelius Grade School, where he was an altar boy, a patrol boy, and a boy scout. In 1958 he graduated from St. Patrick's High School and earned his B.A. from Loyola of Chicago in 1962. After pursuing graduate studies at the University of California in Berkeley, he completed his M.A. in history in 1964 at Xavier University in Cincinnati, Ohio. Then he joined the Jesuits to prepare for the priesthood. His Catholic upbringing provided a foundation for his personal spirituality.

Jesuit Priesthood

About his decision to enter the Jesuit order he said, "This decision was clearly the turning point of (my) adult life." For the first time in his life he was able to appreciate "silence, solitude, nature, self-discipline, personal prayer, community, and the seeds of my creativity" (KFB, 29). It was to be a period of growth and personal transformation that would affect his whole life. His love of solitude, nature, and creativity flourished.

During the time of his studies as a Jesuit scholastic, Ken was involved in more than academic pursuits. In 1967 he began working with Black juveniles at Pedro House in St. Louis. Daily he came in contact with alcoholics and street gangs. He ran a coffee house called "Act II." At this time Ken began to notice the differences in language among the Black youth. He started "to turn over old words that I heard neighbors using in new ways and found new words. I recalled my studies of plantation spirituals as code language bearing the hidden metaphors of resistance and escape" (KFO, 149). Ken's compassionate nature enabled him to minister to the juveniles and street people of St. Louis. He applied his creative energies to developing new words based on sounds, and by 1968 Ken had developed his own "sound poetry."

Experiences continued to change Ken. In 1960 he had proudly waved his Nixon poster on the floor of the Republican convention in Chicago. Eight years later he was teargassed "by Chicago police in Lincoln Park as he protested the Democratic convention's railroading of Eugene McCarthy" (KFB, 28). His would be no ordinary priesthood, and his ministry would take him beyond the walls of conventional Church structures. He was letting go of images of himself, the church, and American society. He asked himself,

> Is the world a better place because I am than because I am not? Am I becoming more rather than less human in my life journey? Such questions are samurai swords cutting swiftly through the layers of masks that I don and they reveal my nakedness (KFB, 27).

The following year Ken moved to Milwaukee, where he organized with the police department to research the Wisconsin prison system. At this time he was teaching minority group history at Marquette High School, helping out at Casa Maria Catholic Worker House, and participating actively in the Vietnam anti-war movement. His social and political involvement was having as much impact on him as was his Jesuit education. His work with the poor, the marginalized, and the oppressed was developing within him a deep sense of compassion.

By 1970 Ken Feit was burned out. Many fellow Jesuits were leaving the order. His intense social activism left him disillusioned with the United States of the 1960s. He developed an attitude of bitterness, righteousness, and humorlessness. It was time to let go of what he was doing. He would have to give birth to a new Ken, and he wasn't sure what that meant.

Clown School

Ken went to visit his friend, Daniel Berrigan, the anti-war Jesuit priest imprisoned in Danbury, Connecticut, for burning draft files. The two discussed the priesthood, political activism, and the idea of the prophet as clown and jester. Berrigan convinced Feit to apply to the Ringling Brothers Clown College in Venice, Florida. Matthew Fox, O.P., later said that passion drove Ken to clown school "to see if, in the midst of wars and rumors of wars, of institutional evil and social sin, he could learn some space, some humor, some transcendence" (MFE, 3). Out of fifteen hundred applicants, Ken was among thirty-six people selected for the training. For seven weeks in 1970, he learned the tricks and trade of clowning and foolishness. His own creativity was transforming him into a new person.

In the fall of 1971, Ken was hired by a Montessori school in Milwaukee as a part-time storyteller, and he listened to and compiled the children's stories. He had also completed his work in sound poetry called *Sound Ways*, which included a book, a teacher's manual, and three audio cassettes published by Loyola University Press.

Ken began making public presentations using his newly acquired clown skills, his sound poetry, and storytelling. He started calling himself an "itinerant fool" and described himself as

> one who verbally, non-verbally, and extra-verbally tells stories, celebrates life, focuses community, proclaims the truth, heals and serves the poor, and is alive to a sense of wonder, mystery and paradox. Relying upon

the traditions of the medieval jester, Old Testament prophet and primitive trickster spirit, he has become concerned with the need for new symbols, myths and rituals to communicate the old wisdom in an age of cultural change (KFC).

The transformation that had affected Ken to the core was now used in performance to challenge, outrage, awaken, and transform his audiences.

Priestly Fool

By 1972 Ken felt the calling of the fool more strongly than the calling of the ordained priesthood.

When the calling of the fool came to me in a conscious way...there was a certain reluctance. I wished to remain on my journey towards priesthood. Somehow I had no choice though. It seemed to me that the full paradox of the fool was something that had embraced me, and now I had to embrace it. I called myself after that "a priestly fool" and left the formal calling of the institutional priesthood and stayed where fools belong—on the edge of the institution, on the periphery, the desert, the mountaintop, the wilderness, the garbage can. That's where fools seem to end up (FFC).

During the summer of 1972, he attended the National Theater for the Deaf in Waterford, Connecticut, and learned American Sign Language (Ameslan). Later he combined Ameslan with mime techniques to produce original sign-mime performances of Japanese haiku and Amerindian myths using his hands.

From 1972 through 1977, Ken Feit's performances took him throughout the United States, Canada, and Europe. In 1974 he began calling himself Wisconsin's "state fool". In March 1975 the Canadian province of Alberta named him its provincial fool for the month. He wrote, "I use the metaphor of the fool, because in history and tradition, the fool has been the enigma, the paradox, the combination of opposites. The fool was the only one who could speak the truth" (JKF). In September 1976 he accepted an appointment as Fool-In-Residence at Barat College in Lake Forest, Illinois. He performed at universities, schools, churches, parks, hospitals, prisons, playgrounds, community theaters, and coffee houses throughout the country. He appeared in over fifty cities in twenty-eight states and five Canadian provinces. By his own recollection, he never stayed in any one place more than two weeks. He did not always find traveling easy.

> I find my vocation as a clown/fool sometimes to be a lonely one, and I am drawn by an itinerant and solitary life-style to transform my loneliness into solitude. There are times when I would rather settle down and raise bees like Virgil, but I know in my heart that I am responding to a call and that there is white-hot passion when I cooperate with my vision. And so I dance (KFL, 10).

As an "itinerant fool" he lived up to his calling. He viewed traveling as a "personal art form and meditation" and saw his vocation "more clearly as awakening new symbols, myths, and rituals in an age of cultural change" (KFB, 30). Traveling was one of several art meditation forms that Ken practiced as a clown and a troubadour.

World Traveler

By 1977 Ken had expanded his itinerary. He embarked on a series of worldwide journeys to meet other fools, offer performances, listen to storytellers in various cultures, and learn all that he could from sages, shamans, magicians, clowns, priests, and jesters. "His models were the itinerant Indian ascetic, the medieval scholar-performer, and the eighth-century Irish monk of the *peregrinatio* for whom travel was revelation, an abandonment to a future known only to God" (JFC, 17). In the fall of 1977, he toured India, Nepal, and Sri Lanka for four months; in 1978 West Africa for four months; in 1979 eighteen countries in South Asia and the Far East for seven months; in 1980 the Near East including Turkey, Israel, and Egypt for four months. He was, fortunately, stateside when his father died in Chicago in April of 1980. He attended the funeral services and added his own farewell.

In 1981 Ken planned to tour South America, the only continent he had not visited. In July he offered a two-week workshop at Dominican College in San Rafael, California. On August 6 Ken performed at the national Clown, Mime, Puppetry and Dance Ministry Workshop in Berkeley, California. Then in order to support the striking air traffic controllers, he decided to drive to his next performance in Mankato, Minnesota. Traveling through the night with a friend who was sleeping in the back seat, Ken fell asleep. The car veered off the road near Heber City, Utah. Ken Feit died in that accident on August 8, 1981, with a plane ticket in his pocket. His friend was uninjured.

At the funeral in Chicago, Ken was eulogized by Matthew Fox, O.P., as "an ordinary man with an extraordnary imagination," who had confided "to at least one friend that he felt his death would come 'on the road'" (MFE, 3). Ken, the fool, had traveled on his final journey.

Major Contributions

For ten years Ken Feit was involved in the performing arts ministry. His workshops and appearances delighted and amused his audiences, but he also challenged and outraged audiences by what he did and said. He understood his role as prophet. He was not afraid to enter into the pain of issues—death, war, aging, violence, sexuality—and transform them in order to promote healing. "I think people take me more seriously," he said, "now that I'm a fool" (JBF, 4). As a priestly fool, he gathered community, entered into mystery and paradox, and celebrated life and death. Ken developed many talents as a performer: clowning, mime, juggling, puppetry, music, and storytelling. In this respect, he was like many other performers, but different in his insight and imagery.

After listening to stories from people around the world, Ken developed storytelling in special ways. But he also contributed three original techniques to "healing/awakening theater" as he called it. His sound poetry, sign-mimes, and the Fool's Mass were unique developments.

Sound Poetry

His work among the Black youth of St. Louis led him to restructure language. This was a two-part process as he saw it.

> Sound poetry basically is concerned with two processes—word-melting and object-becoming. The first process consists in reducing a word by constant repetition to its basic sound/feeling components. This is similar to the effect of chanting a mantra or reciting the rosary. The point is...to flow with the sounds...Word-melting in short is a peek beneath the mask of conventional meaning into the "soul" of a word—primal, mysterious, transforming...Object-becoming is concerned with breaking down conventional word/meaning associations, but from a different perspective. The purpose is to become an object and to discover the sound/word that expresses your new identity (KFO, 152).

This approach to object-becoming and word-melting enabled him to develop many new words—"robuncia" (bathtub), "flongerine" (bathroom), "zachata" (caterpillar), "drazhmeera" (wind whispering through a tropical rain forest), and "jijilakoralee" (monkey). Creating new words led naturally into a new language. This was expanded into his book, *Sound Ways*.

Following are two examples of Ken's sound poems. The appropriate method to appreciate them is to read the poem aloud twice, and then read the explanation. Finally, read the poem aloud again. (For other examples, see *Sound Ways*.)

> whir-rur-rur-rur-rur-rur-rur-rur-rur-rur
> kruk!
> a-a-a-a-ah theerrbeeee!

Explanation: There is a lawn mower munching along the grass (whir-rur-rur). Then it hits a rock and stops (kruk). Then all the unmowed grass with upraised heads and outstretched arms sighs with relief (a-a-ah) (KFS, 7).

> thup-a-thup-a-thup-a-thup-a-thup-a-thup-a-
> fipp!
> bip bip bip bip bip bipbipbipbipbip buh.

Explanation: A little girl is playing with a paddle ball in a steady beat (thup-a-thup-a). Then the rubber band snaps suddenly (fipp). The ball bounces away down the sidewalk with long bounces, then shorter bounces (bip bip bip) until it finally comes to a stop (buh) (KFS, 8).

Sign-Mime

A second creative form developed by Ken Feit is sign-mime. This is a combination of deaf sign language and mime. Ken developed this art form after attending the National Theatre for the Deaf in Connecticut. Sign-mimes are done using the hands.

As you can see from practicing the gestures yourself, the hand talk achieves three effects simultaneously—it physicalizes language (sleep, see, journey, great), suggests different physical centers for cognitive, ethical and emotional expressions (good, spirit, think, mother, bad), and offers a new insight into words which we have learned in unitary terms (dream, death, god, earth, demon)... This process, like deaf sign, offers interesting and sometimes entertaining impressions of the physical world (KFH, 14).

Following are two examples of Ken's sign-mimes. To appreciate them, sign them in silence. Then sign them using the words. One movement flows into another smoothly. Ken chose poems from the Peter Pauper Press haiku series. (For illustrated examples, see "In Praise of Hands.")

> Take this flea.
> He simply cannot jump, and
> I love him for it.
> (Issa)

Capture the essence of the haiku. Using your right hand, place an imaginary flea in the palm of your left hand. Coax it to jump by lightly hitting the underside of your left hand three times with your right hand. Gently bring the flea to your heart using both hands. Now repeat the process to correspond to the poem and recite the words aloud (KFH, 16).

> May the Great Spirit
> work a sunrise
> in your heart.
> (Great Plains Indian Blessing)

From a centered position move both hands out in a small circle to just beyond shoulders (Great). With right hand hold down last two fingers with thumb—first two fingers upright—make a spiral upwards to just above head (Spirit). At chest level open both hands flat facing each other—move hands up and down alternately four times (work). Place right arm on top of left arm—raise right arm slowly with fingers cupped in a circle (sunrise). Point outward with right forefinger (your). Place both hands over heart (heart). Repeat the process corresponding to the blessing and recite the words aloud. (FFC)

Fool's Mass

A third major contribution of Ken Feit to the performing arts ministry was his Fool's Mass. It was an original routine and a product of his creative imagination. It bore little outward resemblance to a real Mass. But it was deeply profound. He referred to his Mass as an extended mime allegory and performed it in silence with Vivaldi's "Four Seasons" as background music.

Ken began by putting on white face, his "vestment," that enabled him to celebrate as a priest-fool. On the floor he placed his battered suitcase to serve as an altar. His presentation was not a parody of the Mass. In silence he evoked reverence, mystery, and awe.

He set before himself a crumpled brown paper bag. He took from the bag some ordinary objects: a balloon, an apple, a banana, a spoon, a handkerchief, paper, and scissors. He greeted each object with a mimed expression of surprise and amazement. He was awed like a child opening a treasure chest of toys.

In turn, each object was examined and played with. Each ordinary object was somehow transformed into something extraordinary. For example, the peel of the half-eaten banana was gently and patiently sewn together with needle and thread in a foolish attempt to return it to its original state. He had exposed the mysteries of life and death. He gently returned it to the crumpled brown bag.

The fool brings forth from a plain shopping bag a beggar's display of the most ordinary objects which, as it were, people every day have before them at all times. He carries these about and shows them off as if there were something wonderful about them in themselves. He requires no special magic or miracle, no supernatural wonder or priestly transubstantiation, for bananas and apples and balloons are already experienced as magic and miracle (CHP, 84).

At Ken's funeral Matthew Fox recalled the last time that Ken had offered his Fool's Mass at the San Rafael workshop. Matt had turned to a woman sitting near him and asked her what it meant to her. She said, "I have been a Roman Catholic all my life; I have been a religious sister for twenty-two years. Today, for the first time, I understand the Mass" (MFE, 3).

Prophet and Mystic

Ken Feit saw himself as a prophet and his priestly fool ministry as a vehicle of prophecy. Walter Brueggemann, in his book *The Prophetic Imagination*, states that "prophetic ministry does not consist of spectacular acts of social crusading or of abrasive measures of indignation. Rather prophetic ministry consists of offering an alternative perception of reality" (WBP, 110).

An alternative perception is what Ken provided through his various crafts. His stories were wrapped in wonder and surprise, while his sound poetry offered a new language and a new form of communication. His sign mimes were creative and original. His Fool's Mass was a celebration, a sharing of the community in mystery, wonder, and awe. It was an opening up of liturgy for those unable to find meaning in contemporary Eucharistic services. He succeeded in transforming the ordinary into something extraordinary.

At the same time, Ken Feit was a twentieth-century mystic. The Protestant philosopher, William Ernest Hocking, called the mystical experience an "apprehension of the presence of God" that was available to everyone as "an awareness of the underlying unity of the world". He concluded that "the prophet is the mystic in action; the mystic is the prophet in reflection and worship" (MFW, 425).

Through travel, silence, street people, sound poetry, creativity and the Fool's Mass, Ken Feit experienced the unity of life and the presence of God. His Jesuit education offered both time and situations for solitude and reflection. Social and political action with and for the poor and oppressed—the anawim—enabled him to encounter God in others. On his travels he shared prophetic and mystical experiences with peoples of many cultures. Ken transformed the perception of ordinary things and created new symbols, myths, and meanings for a world in transition to a new paradigm.

Ken Feit's life parallels the paths of creation spirituality. In his early years at home and school he learned about himself, his talents and gifts, and the original blessing that he was. The time of his social and political activism provoked an emptying that caused burn-out, disillusionment, and bitterness. Following that period of letting go, he experienced a breakthrough—the clown, mime, storyteller, sound poet, itinerant and priestly fool who used those art forms as meditation. By offering workshops and performances Ken used his creativity for transformation—healing, awakening and empowering many others—the anawim, the common people, children, the poor— to see the world and themselves in new ways. As a co-creator, Ken made his life a work of art.

Ken Feit was a mystic and a prophet for our times. As a priestly fool, he touched something inside people and transformed them with what he called "the sacrament of laughter." He reverenced life and all creation. His dream was to be dispensable and to have fools take over his job as healer and teacher. No one can replace Ken Feit. But clowns, mimes, jesters, fools and even priests, can transform his dream into a reality.

This book is an attempt to capture some of the spirit of Ken Feit. It is like trying to capture bubbles. The text is arranged into sections based on the roles Ken lived out. Each page is divided into sense lines to offer an opportunity for reflection and inspiration. A few of his stories are recorded to demonstrate what can be done with storytelling. The final section is a collection of some of the activities that Ken developed. The purpose of the book is not to copy exactly what Ken did, but to take inspiration from his work to develop one's own clown, fool, storyteller, mime, or sound poet. Thus Ken's ministry will continue to inspire and challenge people to become both more foolish and more human.

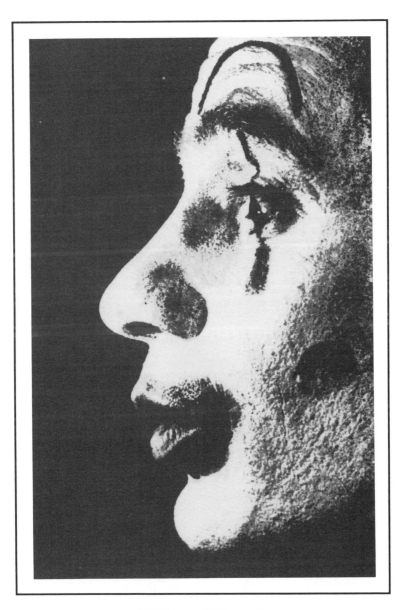

The Fool

Good friend, grasshopper,
will you play the caretaker
for my little grave?

Issa
(KFF)

When I speak of celebration of life,
 I think of death as well as life,
 because of a fear we have of death.
But what we should be afraid of is
 deadness, and not death. (ROF)

The fool is vitally concerned with celebrating life and death. His enemy is deadness—living death. Death has passion and the promise of rebirth; deadness promises ennui, boredom, apathy. The fool's celebration involves excess or abstinence; it is never efficient except in its final end of breaking down old forms and generating new ones. (KFP)

Living in a youth-oriented culture,
    as we do,
we have to find a different way
    of looking at death—
    a way of celebrating it
    and appreciating it.
One has to accept death first
    if one is really going to live. (PLF)

I light a match—the wood dies.
    The flame is born.
I blow it out—the flame dies.
    The smoke is born. (FFC)

To see the ordinary extraordinarily
    (or intraordinarily)
        is the essence of wonder
   and with this vision objects transmute. (KFR)

I blew a bubble explaining its sacredness to me.
It is round, "empty," a window, a mirror,
a rainbow (filled with dancing colors),
short-lived, floating between heaven and earth
and filled with human breath—
a perfect symbol for humankind.

Then it bursts into nothingness/everythingness.

Throughout my journey I blew bubbles
reflecting upon illusion and reality
and gazing at the uniqueness
of each bubble dance. (KFM)

How often we overlook the levels of meaning implicit in a simple gesture. The bubble metaphor is a case in point. In my own clowning sometimes I blow up a bubble, pop it, blow up another, pop it, and then ponder the mystery of what happens to the bubble. Finally I punish the popping finger and blow up another bubble which I swallow. Then I slowly inflate until I pop.

For me this is a symbolic recapitulation of genesis (breath filling the formless substance with life), death (the *digitis Dei* popping the creature), incarnation (the creator swallowing the creature and becoming one with it), crucifixion (the creator-creature bursting in its creatureliness), and resurrection (rediscovering myself as creator with a special compassion for creatures). (KFH)

When I swallowed the bubble,
    it was the Incarnation—
    in a sense,
    Creator becoming Creature. (CTK)

Fools propose other realities
    and invite you
into other parts of yourself. (JTV)

An important archetype for the creative human being
    is the fool or contemporary clown.
The clown's craft is ancient and honorable
    (philosopher, jongleur, galliard, jester)
    and like the prophet sometimes
    success is measured in rejection,
    derision and crucifixion.
The fool performs a sacred role in the community—
    the mirror to the people
    of their ethic and possibilities,
    a teller of truth standing naked in the marketplace
    and confronting the powerful
    with playful disorder,
    a beggar, a storyteller, a magician.
Few things are more awesome than
    a clown let loose in the streets. (UBK)

The fool is a marginal person—
one who stands on the edge of the market place
and comments on the human and divine condition
    through stories, song, puppetry, mask, silence,
    and other expressions.
That does not preclude the fool from being human.
This requires that the fool listen carefully
to each nuance and observe each moment
    of the human dance,
    for play and replay in the mirror of exaggeration.
(KFL)

We fools merely probe playful possibilities,
  mirror ridiculous realities,
  and retreat behind our motley
  with a twinkle in our eye.
Don't take us (or yourself) too seriously. (KFO)

This foolish freedom, won at considerable cost,
　　holds the paradox of the clown...

Within this convention the clown enters another world
　　and becomes a bridge
　　between divine and human,
　　between extraordinary and ordinary—
　　a revelation. (KFL)

The fool appears in every culture in many guises
and in each instance embodies paradox—
order and chaos,
wisdom and stupidity,
prophecy and madness,
fertility and impotence. (KFR)

The key word is paradox—
    the reconciliation of such
    apparent contradictions as
    life/death, male/female, old/young,
    order/chaos, full/empty, dark/light, common/rare.

As a fool, I sidestep the either/or choices of logic
    and choose both.
Thereby I see every moment as
    double-edged,
    bitter-sweet,
    grave-merry. (KFL)

As a clown/fool I have a special language
   to express the vision of paradox.

The mask of whiteface covers my mask of flesh,
   enabling me to uncover my inner self.

No longer confined by convention and laws,
   I can defy physical and social gravity
   through fantasy, transformation,
   sheer roguishness or naivete. (KFL)

My own fool is historically and culturally connected
with my roots as a Westerner and Christian, but I am
convinced that the archetype is more universal than
either. It embraces
>sacred clowns of the Native American,
>the Sufi dervish,
>Hausa yakamansi,
>Zen monk,
>Jewish badhan,
>Russian Salia,
>primitive trickster,
>medieval jester,
>and a myriad of other people
>(children, artists, mystics, dreamers,
>primitives, prophets, shamans, and
>madmen and women) who live intuitively,
>>symbolically,
>>passionately and
>>paradoxically.
>>(KFL) ·

I am interested in the fool
    as an agent of spirituality.
Unless we become as fools,
    we cannot really be wise. (JTV)

The fool's discernment is always directed toward wonder and mystery. These are found in the Zen fool in the "given" circumstances and objects surrounding him, or for the *koshare* in the "shadows" that he finds, creates, and enters. In all instances this discernment is expressed in paradox, the transcendent reconciliation of exclusives (life-death, night-day, male-female, good-bad, right-wrong, intellect-intuition). This path of transcendence is most vividly realized physically in the circus clown's ritual of making up, a deliberate self-abandonment to the spirit of prophetic folly. (KFP)

If much is demanded of the clown much is offered in return. The very act of "making-up" involves him in the process of self-discovery and self-transcendence. The clown by abandoning personal history and entering the realm of ritual celebration undertakes a personal vision-quest beyond the mask of flesh and the weaponry of words. He enters into the inner face, into the language of non-words and ultimately into silence and stillness. Everything is inverted. The whiteface by masking the clown in anonymity unmasks his true identity and permits him to reveal himself as never before. But even this identity is transcended in the ritual of folly for the clown embodies a freedom that is simultaneously threatening and inviting. In whiteface the clown is a true outlaw, beyond class and caste. He can break all of the social conventions and speak the truth like the medieval jester. Ultimately this is his undoing since society has a limited tolerance for the truth. (KFP)

I don't consider myself
an accomplished fool.

That's the vision
I'm working toward.

Me, I rejoice in my littleness. (BHF)

The Priest

Since my house burned down,
I now own a better view
of the rising moon.

Massahide
(KFF)

The clown celebrates life
and the priest celebrates life.

The clown is eternal
and so is the priest. (TJS)

As far as priesthood goes, I would say "yes." I call myself a priest. I also call myself a shaman, or a healer in that sense. But what I mean by priest is really a generic notion. I think of a priest as a healer, as a storyteller, as a celebrant, but not simply of pleasure, of pain as well. I think of a priest as a former of community, though the person doesn't always live in that community. I think of a priest as one who is a discerner of wonder and mystery and paradox. And always a servant—one who attempts to take the power that one has and empower other people with it. (FFC)

The term "priestly fool" is used to describe that person,
　　　male or female,
　　who is a discerner of wonder, mystery and paradox;
　　who celebrates life and death;
　　who is a storyteller and listener;
　　who is a focuser of community
　　　　(though frequently living on the periphery
　　　　of the community);
　　who is a proclaimer of the truth
　　　　(verbally and non-verbally);
　　who is a servant and healer of the poor
　　　　(powerless); and
　　who resymbolizes, reritualizes, and remythologizes
　　　　for the tribe. (KFP)

The priest fool focuses the people around a new (and very old) vision. As tribal ritualizer he calls the people to renew themselves through the ancient myth relived. He tells the old story again and in doing so the people reexperience it—alone, with one another, and in communion with the event itself. The *koshari* call forth the *kachinas*, the *heyokas* summon the thunder spirits, and the circus clown salutes the virtuosi. Each is *pontifex* between people and ultimate mystery. (KFP)

In yet another sense the clown performs the priestly function of reconciliation. To a circus audience the virtuosi (acrobats, jugglers, equestrians, lion tamers, aerialists) are awesome, unapproachable mysteries of human possibility. In their courage and dexterity they are simultaneously pinnacles of human achievement and reproaches to the masses for their own mediocrity. The onlooker responds, "How amazing!" and "I could never do that." Suddenly the clown appears and falls on her face. The onlooker laughs and responds, "I could do that. Anybody could do that." The circus clown as Everyman bridges the gap between the virtuosi and the people just as the *koshare* clown bridges the Hopi villagers and the *kachina* spirits. She is the intermediary that makes tangible, believable, celebratable the wondrous events that surround them. And her rubric is laughter. (KFP)

In the clown's sacred freedom (urgency) to speak the truth and in the ensuing laughter lie the mystery of his priesthood. His clowning basically is a mirror to the people of their own ethic and identity. In laughing at him they laugh at themselves. In laughing at themselves they laugh with themselves. In laughing with themselves they forgive themselves for they perceive their own frailty. God can only forgive them when they have forgiven themselves by first acknowledging their absurdity. Thus the clown serves as a general confessor to the people, first by taking on their sins (absurdities, frailties, hypocrisies) in his clowning and then by absolving them through their own laughter. It is the mystery of crucifixion and resurrection reenacted. (KFP)

By silent imitation and exaggeration
    I can mirror the world around me—
    the foibles of human society.

In laughing at me, others consciously or unconsciously
    laugh *at* themselves,
    then *with* themselves.

Thereby, they acknowledge their own foolishness and
    forgive themselves through
    the sacrament of laughter. (KFL)

According to the ancient conventions of make-up,
   when a clown "puts on whiteface"
   something magical happens,
   like the magic of the Eucharistic prayer.

In whiteface the clown loses sexual identity,
   becoming neither male nor female,
   but assuming the guise of one or both.

The clown also loses any personal history
   and is ageless, being neither old nor young
   but transcending time.

As such, the clown belongs to no race
   or cultural grouping,
   but lives on the edge of all societies,
   defying containment by law, mores, and reason.
   (KFP)

The whiteface, motley, and other conventions
    serve the functions of
    priestly vestments or shamanic power objects.
Personally, I must spend 30 minutes
    in silent meditation
    before beginning a performance, and during it
    I have only peripheral awareness of myself.
It's as though I am God's puppet. (KFL)

Like the priest who commits himself through vows to service in the community, the clown realizes her ministry of folly by a similar kenosis, one that affects her physical being. In whiteface, the clown may not use her ordinary voice; she must remain silent or exaggerate her voice. She may not eat, drink, or smoke unless it has a comic effect (like a rubber hot dog or an exploding cigar). Once made up, the clown may not eliminate or make love, nor may she feel pain; hence the laughter that pratfalls and thwacks provoke. Ultimately the clown may not even die since she is always expected to bounce back buoyantly from each mishap. The specter of a clown seriously injured from a fall or mauling, lying helplessly in the center ring, is almost sacrilegious. It contradicts every expectation. It is no small matter to "vest" for the "liturgy of wonder" that occurs under the Big Top or in the streets. The principal celebrant must forfeit tongue, stomach, lungs, bladder, genitals, nerve endings, even her psychic identity and the power to end the sacrifice by ritual death. (KFP)

Service is rendered to the powerless (the poor) through the power of the fool's freedom. These poor ones are the true masters of the servant-priest-fool and they command his service. Their powerlessness assumes many forms— physical, economic, intellectual, psychological, spiritual. In sharing the mystery of freedom which comes through faith, the fool empowers the powerless (or rather they empower themselves in his presence) so that they too serve. Ultimately each person perceives herself or himself as powerful and powerless in one respect or other so that the fool's dance becomes one of interdependent service. In this way Christians see Christ as their realized fool of history, powerful enough to become the suffering servant of humanity. Through his suffering service all realize their own power to serve. (KFP)

Ultimately the priest-fool's life itself is the lesson and her word-actions are corollaries culminating in silence-stillness. Words or actions are meaningless unless they are separated by silences or stillnesses between them, and unless they proceed from the inner silence and stillness (attention) of one person to that of another. The lesson of the fool is obedience or open-earedness. Her speech is a sharing of silences as her deed is a sharing of stillnesses. (KFP)

If it helps to make fools out of priests, may it also make priests out of fools, and artists out of both; for the artful, playful, and sacred share a common domain. Art, play, and prayer are the only human activities that are totally purposeless yet absolutely meaningful (unlike work which is thoroughly purposeful but usually meaningless). Thus the fool and priest join the artist in a conspiracy of meaning. (KFP)

Everyone is called upon
    to celebrate his or her own folly.
Everyone is called to be impractical:
    it's pretty foolish to have children,
    when you consider all that's involved.
Turning the other cheek is foolish.
Christianity is a religion of folly. (JSP)

To be a Christian is to be a fool
in the sense that
one must confront authority with the truth. (TJS)

One of the tragedies of the Church is
    its humorlessness.
It's too dead serious.

Without humor there is very little hope,
    and we're trying to engender new values.

I guess I wouldn't want to be a part
    of a Church that couldn't dance. (GGC)

I must offer my fool's mass
    in the camp
and celebrate the victory of life and death
    over deadness, apathy, boredom and mediocrity—
the barbed wire and guards
    that pervade our society. (KFR)

The fool's mass is the central act of my life now—
creating sacred space and time,
focusing community,
celebrating wonder, mystery, and paradox,
discerning pain and healing inner wounds,
proclaiming new/old age of hope, and
empowering others to discover and tell their stories.
(KFR)

Henceforth our true language
occupies the space between sounds and movements.

This new language—the true Pentecost—
connects and gives meaning to words and actions
by its openness and readiness to receive.

We become the smiling Buddha,
              the silent Christ.

At that moment our hands simply rest palms up
and we are grasped by a greater reality. (KFH)

In a mime allegory that I do, at one moment
I put a single kernel of popcorn in a spoon.
    Then I put a few drops of oil in the spoon
and hold it over a candle for what seems like
    an eternity (45 seconds)
    waiting for it to pop.
Now, I never know if it is going to pop or not.
    I just have to take that chance.

    To me, that's the wonderful allegory
of the resurrrection.
    The popcorn kernel is a seed that must die
unto itself in the flame of transformation
        in the oil of anointing
        in a spoon that is the crucible
          (a kind of womb/tomb)
        in order to be reborn.

    The popcorn undergoes a literal kind
of transubstantiation.
    It changes color, size, shape, texture.
    It makes an audible and visible pop.
    It is a much more dramatic example
of transubstantiation
    than the words of consecration
    spoken over a piece of bread. (FFC)

My dream is to become totally irrelevant,
    to have fools take over my job.
So, to be dispensable is the goal of a fool—
    of this fool anyway.
That ought to be the goal of every priest too. (FFC)

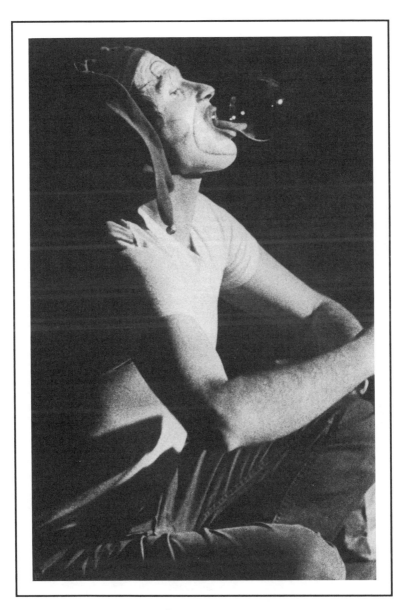

The Storyteller

On the last, long road
when I fall and fail to rise,
I'll bed with flowers.

Sora
(KFF)

I try to get people to think about
    their lives as stories and
    realize they don't know everything
    about themselves.
The rest of their lives is carrying out those stories.

Life would be pretty boring
    if we all knew who we were. (CAP)

I like to hitchhike. Maybe it's because highways are filled with so much empty moving space. What a waste! All those cars with one person in them. The road cries out for life: for tar grazers like me who travel along the road building a pilgrim community where people need each other. To stand on the edge of the highway thumbing a ride is to risk everything, not knowing who, when, why, or how far the ride will come and go. It's impossible to step into a car without becoming friends with the driver. This doesn't happen when I take the bus. It's very difficult to start up a conversation with a fellow passenger. After all, who needs who if everybody's paid for! (KFS)

When you go out in the field and see a herd of cattle grazing, it's so easy to be caught up in the countryness that you might miss the other worlds around. But if you bend down and look closely at a single blade of grass, you'll see another world. You'll see a bunch of tiny insects—aphids—herded together sucking the juices of the single grass blade, filling themselves with grass juice. And if you look long enough, you'll see ants coming close, drawing up alongside the aphids, bending their feelers over them and squeezing them, probing them, stroking them, and drawing juice from them. And the aphid juice is now ant juice. But the ant didn't kill the aphid, it herded him. And so the ant returns to his family with the grass-aphid-ant juice and life goes on.

Only one time, somewhere, maybe everywhere, a cow bends over and chomps a mouthful of grass. And in that single moment it chomps herds and herds of aphids grazing, the ranching, farming ants, and that grass. Down it goes into their stomachs. No longer is it grass juice or aphid juice or ant juice. It's cow juice, milk. And man, antlike, milks the cow, not seeing the aphid or the ant or the field that is a single blade of grass. But if he did, he might say to himself: Maybe this whole planet is a tiny dewdrop on a giant blade of grass in the universe, and there's a giant aphid out there in space bending down about to chomp us and our worldly juices into a new world. There are so many levels to life and we must share them. (KFS)

Did you ever liberate an ice cube?
An ice cube, after all, is water that's kept in prison
    to serve humans' needs by cooling their drinks
    and soothing their headaches.
Well, I sometimes ransom bags of ice cubes
    from gas stations,
        take them to nearby ponds, and let them go
        so they can return
        to their water brothers and sisters. (KFS)

I can't stay in one place very long.
It's the popcorn in me. (JCJ)

Coeur D'Alene Story

Once a woman had twin children who fainted away. Possibly they only slept. Their mother left them in the morning and when she returned in the evening, they were still lying there. She noticed their tracks around the house; therefore she thought they must have come to life and played during her absence. One day she stole on them unseen and found them arguing with each other inside the lodge. One said, "It is much better to be dead." And the other said, "It is better to be alive." When they saw her, they stopped talking, and since then people die from time to time. There are always some being born and some dying at the same time, always some living ones and some dead ones. Had she remained hidden and allowed them to finish their argument, one would have prevailed over the other, and there would have been either no life or no death. (KFC)

The effect of story telling is not only to heal but also to awaken and even outrage as a Zen koan or a Sufi story does. The parables of Jesus are a case in point. They begin with a simple story line then reverse themselves at the very end. Thus the good Samaritan and publican (despised by Jews) are justified while the priest, levite, scribe, and pharisee are condemned, those who work one hour are given the same wage as those who labor for eleven, the shepherd abandons his flock to find the lost sheep, the uninvited are welcomed at the wedding feast and the formerly invited are spurned, and the father welcomes his prodigal son while his obedient older son is unfeasted. Here the storyteller is inviting his listeners to abandon law for spirit, logic for paradox, appearance for reality, externals for essentials, justice for mercy and love. Little wonder that he was crucified. (KFR)

Sufi Story

Once Nasreddin attended a banquet in his ragged clothes and was ejected from the hall. He went home, dressed in fine attire, and returned to the banquet. He was seated at the head table and offered a large portion. He immediately began smearing the food on his clothes. When questioned, he answered, "When I came earlier in poor clothing, I was unwelcome. Now that I am well dressed I am welcome. Apparently it is my clothing that received the invitation. So I am feeding it." (KFJ)

Chinese Story

Once a man was dining with a Chinese doctor when there was a knock at the door. There stood a man with a bandaged head and a bandaged object in his hand. Unwinding his head gauze revealed that his ear was missing; he was holding it in his hand. The doctor, upon examining the ear, sent him away telling him that the ear was too old and withered to sew back on. The man bowed politely and left. An hour later there was another knock at the door. There stood the same man holding a fresh ear in his hand. (KFM)

Puppetry is also an excellent way for telling stories, teaching and counseling. By interacting with one another the hands can mirror conflicts between people. Sometimes we can objectify our own conflicts and resolve them by such a dialogue. Our hands can also call us to accountability when we are trapped by role definitions or social convention. An ever-present Jiminy Cricket, the hand can tap us on the shoulder, slap us in the face, tickle us, or pick us up out of the dumps. (KFH)

Chinese Story

(Ken told this story using an Oriental fan as a prop. At parts in the story it became the sun, the hat, the pipe, and all the other objects mentioned.)

One day old man...wake up...with rise of sun...decide go fishing. So take favorite hat, and pipe and pole and cane ...and make long journey to far away mountain....where water is fresh and fish are many. Old man come to edge of water...he sit down...take off hat...put down cane...throw out line...light pipe...and open small bottle sake. Soon old man grow sleepy and dream begin. In dream old man have great struggle with giant fish in wind and rain. Old man catch fish...bring home to village where he is cornered by elders. Then dream end...old man wake up...find self not in village with elders...but in shallow water...no great fish...only empty bottle sake. So old man smile at self...step out of water...pick up hat...and pipe...and pole and cane...watch setting of sun...and begin journey home.

(from a private video made in Alaska in 1981)

The Princess, the Frog, and the Little Bird

(Ken told this story using his bowed psaltery. Each of the characters and the various noises had a specific sound on the instrument.)

Once upon a time...long, long ago there lived a little princess....One day she heard a knock on the castle wall....She went down the stairs....She slowly opened the door of the castle....There was a little bird....Well, the princess...and the little bird...decided to go for a walk...till they suddenly came to a brook....And right in the middle of the brook was a frog....The princess...and the little bird...and the frog...decided to have a picnic. It was a wonderful, wonderful picnic...until suddenly...they heard the thunder...and the rain....And the wind blew so hard...that the little brook...became a raging torrent. And the princess...was swept into the water. And she cried for help and cried and cried and cried for help. But the little bird...couldn't do anything. But the frog...the frog jumped in the water and swam and swam and swam until he came to the little princess...and very politely he took her hand and swam back to the shore. He took the rest of her too. And set her down. And then wonderfully the thunder...stopped and the rain...stopped. And the wind...became a gentle breeze. And the princess...was so grateful to that frog...that she picked him up and gave him a big...kiss. You know what happened to that frog? Nothing!! He was still a little frog. But he was a happy frog. And he was so happy that he joined the princess...and the little bird...hopping...skipping...jumping... flying, swimming, digging, dancing, and whispering the way back to the castle where they opened the door...ran up the stairs...and lived happily ever after....That's the end.

(from a private video made in Alaska in 1981)

Blackfoot Shaman Story (Smoking-Star)

Our chief led a party against the Cree and invited me to go. The chief was jealous of me. He was a bad man, but I could not refuse. Medicine-bear, the shaman, went with us to give us power. When we reached the Cree country, I was ordered out as a scout. It was dark. As I went along I saw a tepee all by itself. I went up to it quietly and looked in. There was no one in the tepee except a man, his wife, and a little child. The little child could just walk and was amusing itself by dipping soup from the kettle with a small horn spoon. The man and his wife were busy talking and paid no attention to the child. Now the child looked up and saw me peeping through the hole, toddled over to the kettle, dipped up some soup in the spoon and held it to my lips. I drank and the child returned to the kettle for more. In this way the child fed me for many minutes. Then I went away.

As I went along to my own party, I thought to myself, "I do not like to do this, but I must tell my party about this tepee. When they know of it, they will come and kill these people. This little child fed me even when I was spying upon them, and I do not like to have it killed. Well, perhaps I can save the child; but then it would be too bad for it to lose its parents. No, I do not see how I can save them, yet I cannot bear to have them killed."

Blackfoot Shaman Story

I sat down and thought it over. After awhile I went back to the tepee, went in, and sat down. While my host was preparing the pipe, the child began to feed me again with the spoon. After we had smoked, I talked to the man in the sign-language, told him all but that they had been saved by the little child. Then I directed the man to go at once, leaving everything behind him in the tepee.

Never have I forgotten that little child. Some great power was guarding it. Its medicine was strong. Many times have I prayed to that power and sometimes it helped me, but I do not yet know what power it is. Yet somehow I took little interest in war, the child's medicine did that to me. (KFC)

When I am telling stories, I feel that
    I enter a sort of trance state.
I do things that I ordinarily would not do.
    I become caught up.
I am filled with another spirit, another energy.
    I feel like a flute
    that is being blown through.
That is essentially the prophetic
    and revolutionary moment
    to be drawn and driven by another. (FFC)

Akhi, the beggar

Allah!!! (shouted very loudly—and drawn out)

Greetings, strangers. Welcome to the market place. My name is Akhi, and I am a beggar. All day long I sit here in the market place, and I beg. People push and shove. They buy and sell. But Akhi, he sits and begs.

Perhaps you wonder why Akhi is a beggar. Akhi! Why don't you do honorable work, you might think. Maybe you think that. It is a good wonder. I will tell you why I am a beggar. It is because I have a beggar's path. Oh, yes. Each of us is called to a path. And to follow one's path is holy—always. Akhi is called to be a beggar. For Akhi, not to beg would be a sacrilege. So Akhi begs. But he begs with pride.

I have studied for many years. I have practiced and sat at the feet of the Masters. You know, I went to the academy of beggars. Yes. You must beg your way in and beg your way out. It is like the universities in the United States, I understand. Yes, I beg, and I learned from the great Master beggar—from Raul who could beg life into a dead baby, and Abraham who could beg rain upon the desert. They were Master beggars. Akhi, he is a beggar, but he is following a beggar's path. That is the difference.

But why do we beg, you may wonder. I will tell you, It is because of the dance. That is why we beg. Oh, yes, each of us is called to the dance. Yes. We move our prayers as other people move their feet. But there are people—there are people in the market place who are afraid of the dance. They cling to their life, to their possessions, oh, to their reputation. Oh, yes. And they are weighed down with all of them. They cannot move. It's like human camels, like stones. What a pity these people do not know how to dance.

Akhi, the beggar

But that is why we have beggars. We sit in the market place, and when they come we say, "Oh, give us a piece of bread, give us a coin in the name of Allah." And if they do, if they reach into their pockets and give us a coin, they are lighter—maybe they can dance. You see. You see. Beggars try to make people lighter so they can dance.

And so begging is holy. Oh, yes. But you smile. You say, "Akhi, are you joking with me?" What?? Cannot a beggar joke with you? What do you think? You probably wonder, "Oh, Akhi, you take our coins and spend them on yourself." Ha !!

You think I want to be a human camel like you? No! Ha. I will tell you a secret. Your bread we feed to the birds. Your coins—well, that is another matter. I have friend, Amat, from Baghdad. Oh, yes. Every holy day he takes the coins you give him. He puts them in his purse, and he goes to the holy river, to the Euphrates, and throws them in the water to listen to the splash. It is his weakness—the splash. It is also his prayer. Akhi, he climbs the first level of the holy mountain every day at noon and takes the silver and gold coins you give him and throws them at the sun–and watches them glisten–and listens to them sing as they dance down the mountain. It is Akhi's weakness, Akhi's prayer. And why should it not be so? The coins you have come from the holy mountain, come from the holy river. Should they not return there? We beggars, we are middle men. We help with the cash flow. We know you will go back to the mountain and river searching for them again. And so it is. We are content. It makes for the dance.

Akhi, the beggar

Ha! I will tell you something. One day—one day—Allah may it be soon—one day everybody will be dancing. Oh, what a day that will be. If you go in the market place—you go looking—you will see our rugs, our rags, our bowls. But you will not see us. The beggars will be gone, because our path will be over. Yes. The dance will be here. We will not be necessary. Allah, bring this day closer. So many camels. So many camels. Ask yourself, "Am I too heavy? Can I dance today?" If you can't, you know what you must do. And maybe, maybe you are not following your path yet. What is your path? What is your path, stranger? Maybe one of you is called to be a beggar. You could do worse, you know. Yes. Yes, you could go to the academy and study with Abraham and with Raul. Yes. And you could sit here with me in the market place. And together we could beg. How good it would be. What is your path? What is your path? Are you finding it? I hope so.

May Allah guide you. But now I must go back to my begging. May Allah watch over you. May you find your path. And may you join me in the dance. Praised be Allah! Praised be his children!! Praised be the universe!

Allah!!! (shouted very loudly—and drawn out)

(PFC)

Cleo the pregnant woman

Howdy! My name's Cleo. This here's my baby. T'aint my only baby. T'aint my first baby. I have me other babies, too. Lots of babies and lots of fathers. Cleo, she like variety. Had me a baby I called Egypt—on account it build blocks and play with things. Had me a baby I called Rome—on account it roam around lots, build lots of roads, and got mighty powerful. It's kind of a bully, my baby Rome. Sometimes it beat up on the other babies.

One day Rome just up and died. Me and Egypt, we went to the funeral. I cried powerful lot that day. But Egypt just snickered. Couldn't understand why it is my baby snicker when another baby dies. It tears a mother's heart sometimes. Had me a baby I called England—loved to play in the water.

I have me this here baby too. Wanna tell ya somethin'. Sometimes, sometimes when I'm layin' in bed on my back, I feel an awful kickin' in my belly, and I say "What my baby tryin' to tell me?" And sometimes I close my eyes and try to sleep and I say, "Oh, I have a turrible, turrible pain in my head. What's it mean?" Don't know. So one day I went to my friend, the fortune-teller lady. She a conjure woman; she a herb lady; she a powerful good friend I said,

—Good mornin', fortune-teller lady.
*Good mornin', Cleo.
—I come to see you, fortune-teller lady.
*Don't gotta be a fortune-teller lady to tell that. I see ya plain as day, Cleo.
—What I means, fortune-teller lady, is I got me a problem.
*The problem in your belly, huh, Cleo?

Cleo the pregnant woman

—That's right, fortune-teller lady. That's where it is.
Can ya help me? Sometimes I lay on my back, I feel a
kickin' in my belly. Sometimes I close my eyes, I feel
a pain in my head.
*Well. This sounds serious. Set yourself down. I'll
check ya over.

And I did set myself down, and she raise up my dress,
and she put her hand on my belly and she feels around
real good and she say,

*Cleo, is your baby something else!
—I know that fortune-teller lady.
*I mean it's something "else" else!
—Whatcha mean?
*I mean this here baby's gonna be strong.
—Stronger than Rome?
*That's right! This here baby gonna be rich!
—Richer than Egypt?
*Uh-huh. This here baby gonna travel a lot!
—More than England?
*That's right!
—Well that's wonderful, fortune-teller lady. I'm much
obliged for what you tell me.
*Not so fast, Cleo! You didn't let me finish.
—Whatcha got to say?
*Just this. Your baby gonna be strong but gonna beat
up on the babies what it don't like.
—No!
*Yeah-us. Your baby gonna be rich and have lots of
food, but keep it for its own mouth.
—No!

Cleo the pregnant woman

*Yeah-us. Your baby gonna travel lots. But its eyes gonna be mostly closed.

—No!

*Yeah-us. Cleo, I don't wants to tell ya these things, but I gots to. It's my job. I feel it in your belly. I got to tell ya.

—Tell me, fortune-teller lady, ain't der a goodness in my baby?

*There's a goodness. Your baby's a good baby, but it got a streak of meanness too.

—But there's goodness?

*And meanness!

—And goodness.

*And meanness.

—(whispered) And goodness.

 Tell me somethin', fortune-teller lady.

*Whatcha wanna know, Cleo?

—What name should I give my baby? Huh?

And she put her hand on my belly again and she go into a swoon and she say,

*Call your baby, call your baby...Cleo, call your baby—America!

—America?

*America!

—I never heard that name before.

*I just made it up.

—But why America?

*On account of it's genuine kind—and that's Amer.
 But it's mean too. And that's Ca!

—Can't I just call my baby, Amer?

*You forget the Ca, and you get a kick in the teeth from your own baby. You understand?

Cleo the pregnant woman

—I understand. It be America.

*Ameri-ca!

—America!

*Ameri-ca! That's right.

—Tell me somethin', fortune-teller lady. I'm feared with whatcha say. Should I have this baby, or should I stop it in my belly?

*I can't tell you what to do. Cleo. I can't tell you. You gots to do whatcha gots to do! You're the mother. You'll know. No one can tell ya.

—I reckon you're right, fortune-teller lady. I reckon you're right. No one can tell me what to do. Thank ya. Much obliged.

*Don't you fret now, Cleo. You're a strong woman and a good woman. I'll stand by ya.

—I know you will, fortune-teller lady. I'm much obliged.

*That's all right. Now you go on home. If you need me, you call, and I'll be there.

—I know you will. Us—us ladies got to stand tall together. Right, fortune-teller lady?

*Right, Cleo! Tall together! We stand! Right! I'll see you, Cleo.

—See you, fortune-teller lady.

So. Y'all see. Here old Cleo sit with America in her belly. She don't know what to do. Sometimes I say, "I'm gonna have me this baby." Yep. Don't care what. Sometimes I say, "No-o-o way! What might my baby do to my other children? To China, and Vietnam, and Russia? And what might they do to my baby, America?" It frightens me. It frightens me powerful.

Cleo the pregnant woman

Don't know what to do. Don't know. What would y'all do if'n you had America in your belly? Would you have it, or would you stop it? I needs help. I don't know. How about you, mister? Would you have the baby, or would you stop it? Keep it, then. You, mister? You'd have the baby too! How about you? Don't know. How about you? Y'all mighty brave with Cleo's baby. Yeah.

That's the way it is. Maybe you're tellin' me somethin'. Maybe I should just go ahead and have my baby. Reckon I will. It ain't easy bein' a single parent, you know. I need baby sitters. Day care's goin' up. I'm gonna have to have some help from you folks. Maybe some of you will babysit for America for me when I'm workin'. Yeah, maybe you will. I gots to warn you. My baby got a mean streak in it. Sometimes you gotta wop America in the butt for its own good. But be good to my baby too. It's a nice baby, a mighty nice baby. Well. You take care. I'm gonna call you when my baby comes out. You be sure of that. You be mighty sure. America, you so little, so tiny. The fortune-teller lady, she says such big things for you. I don't even know if you're a boy or a girl. Oh, no. Well, my baby's sleepin'. Y'all be quiet while I put my baby to sleep. Be quiet. (PFC)

When I am a musician,
    God is a no-string bass.
When I am a child,
    God is the thumb that nurtures me.
When I am Cleo, the pregnant woman,
    God is who gives me courage to have my baby.
When I am an Indian,
    God is the great mystery.
When I am a beggar,
    God is the ultimate dancer.
And when I am a fool,
    God is who blows the greatest bubble. (CAP)

The core of my folly is
    not eating flowers
    or riding unicycles.
It is story-telling,
    myth-making, and
    word-making. (JDS)

The Prophet

Icicles and water—
old differences dissolved...
drip down together.

Teishitsu
(KFF)

I wanted to be a clown
so I could understand
the prophetic role of humor
and learn the ritual of celebration. (TJS)

In an individualistic society
    it is important to discover community
    and to regain a lost sense of ritual
    in making our journeys with
    that community. (CAP)

The fool is often a lonely wanderer,
    without a tribe or family,
    yet this is his calling,
    and when immersed in his folly,
    he experiences a special intimacy
    with those who join him;
    promises implicitly are exchanged
    and a kinship forms—
    folly is contagious. (KFC)

I direct my actions toward those
    who are afraid of themselves,
      locked into routines, trapped, despairing. (MHF)

All I'm trying to do is find
    universal symbols that kind of tickle people
    to the threshold of a personal query,
    and just leave it there. (CTK)

It is an exciting and awe-ful moment
> when people struggle to express
> the familiar in unfamiliar ways.

Slaves and prisoners of war have known such moments.
So have visitors to foreign cultures
or inmates of total institutions like
prisons,
seminaries,
or armies. (KFH)

In a flash I saw two visions of language like the cities of Augustine. One was intuitive, process, personal, marginal and the other was conceptual, static, conventional, mainstream.

In the first city lived children, primitives, dreamers, artists, cripples, seniles, the poor and powerless, mystics, madmen and fools.

The other world was peopled by the rest of society— adults, rationalists, professionals, skeptics, the economically secure and powerful, healthy, civilized, and buffoons.

Between the two cities there were constant exchanges as children became "educated" or adults became senile, as fortunes were won or lost, as sickness, madness, faith, or folly were cured or caused.

That night I went home and stayed up all night creating my own language—sound poetry. (KFO)

I want to unhinge the mind
  from the definition of things
  it has been civilized into.

The things I do are magical
  and certainly foolish.
After all, if most people did them,
  they would lose their jobs. (CAP)

The freedom a clown embodies
　is totally inviting and threatening.
Her very presence is a statement of liberation
　that reveals to the spectators
　their own chains,
and it is far more tempting
　to capture and abuse the clown
　than to become one.
But the clown is legion;
　her folly is latent in all of us. (KFC)

I perceive good and evil in myself and the world but see the greatest danger for our society in the decline of excellence and fidelity in relationships, work, self-regard and nature-regard, loss of faith and disconnectedness from history and tradition.

Institutions have become the new idols
conferring through
      their high priests (bosses/executive boards)
      salvation (career advancement),
      grace (pay raises/corporate profits),
      absolution (union/company policy),
      a sacred language (jargon),
      service (seductive advertising),
      and immortality (the ability of successful
      institutions to outlive their members). (KFB)

There are only two kinds of people in this world—
    fools and buffoons.
Buffoons are
    those who either take life too seriously, or
    those who live too frivolously.
Fools are
    those who can be both
    merry and grave. (DPF)

Fools live in hope,
and if they are going to work
in a situation that seems hopeless
they need the sense of folly. (JLR)

The fool knows no laws,
    not even the law of time.
The fool laughs at the mores of society.
    That's why people feel threatened
    by the fool. (ROF)

The clown isn't afraid—
    he can bridge social conventions
    without being innocuous.
The clown is the ideal motif for speaking in new ways.
    He's timeless, sexless, raceless.
    He gains powers and loses them. (MHF)

The fool is the lord of disorder
creating new order
on the edge of society. (MBC)

In Christianity there is a root
between the prophet, priest and fool.

Jesus was a fool
in the sense of
one who speaks the truth
from a position of vulnerability,
the powerless one before power. (JLR)

The most fundamental revolution of all
is self-transcendent delight in the unexpected. (KFM)

We are a people alienated from our selves—
    our hands, faces, bodies.

By listening to ourselves
    we awake the word in sound and movement.
This step of self-discovery and self-expression
    is intermediate, however, to a still greater step,
    the moment of self-transcendence
    when we find sound and movement unnecessary.

The Word is obvious
and so we surrender to it
in silence and stillness. (KFH)

I am attempting to celebrate
   the convergence of spirituality,
   aesthetics, and therapy by means of
   words, sounds, movements, silences and stillnesses.
It is part of a larger question,
   namely, how can we discover viable symbols,
   myths and rituals in our tumultuous times?
My odyssey takes me into tradition,
   primitive folk symbols and myths,
   childhood and fantasy.
It is but one of many possible efforts, and
   it is the basis of my personal vocation. (UWM)

Folly is not something that one chooses.
Folly chooses you like prophecy,
    and it's not always a happy choice.

The Old Testament prophets dreaded
    being chosen and often tried to avoid it
    as Jonah did, as Isaiah and Jeremiah did.

They know that prophets get thrown into pits
    or chased into caves
    or swallowed by whales
    or crucified.
Similar things happen to fools too. (FFC)

Basically,
I am concerned with celebration
as a subversive activity. (KFR)

The Mystic

Live in simple faith
just as this trusting cherry
flowers, fades and falls.

Issa
(KFF)

I am concerned with engendering
    a sense of wonder, mystery, and paradox in people,
    and helping them take delight in the mystery
    within them and around them.
I want people to realize a sense of the Divine
    within themselves. (BGR)

We must begin with a sense of wonder and reverence for the family of all living things. Then perhaps we can discover a language everybody can speak and understand. I think that the American Indians came close to discovering such a language. They worshiped in the temple of nature: the plains, forests, mountains, lakes, or deserts. They worshiped the spirit of the sun and honored the protecting spirits of the snake, spider, elk, bear, eagle, and buffalo. They smiled at the friendly spirits of the coyote, jay bird, porcupine, and turtle. They kept all of their protecting spirits close to them by carrying totems and singing songs. Before and after a hunt, feast, or a war party, they praised their spirits in dance, paint, chant, and costume. They made them promises and promises were kept.

All life was sacred. Fire was full of mystery and sacred tobacco was offered in thanksgiving. Gift-giving, friendliness, sharing land, and families living and working together were all important. Life was a journey and time was now, always now. Mystery was everywhere, within and without. (KFS)

My totems are the spider
    (weaving from within her ephemeral
    web-mandala, shield, mask, home,
    trap, fantasy, window, vision, story)
            the turtle
    (carrying home on back and proceeding slowly,
    cautiously on land and in water), and
            the bee
    (collecting and alchemically transforming
    pollen into ambrosia,
    cross-fertilizing and networking fields
    of stationary flowers). (KFB)

My vocation is to make
    extraordinary things ordinary,
    and
    ordinary things extraordinary. (MFE)

After a while you will begin to discern
    different levels of silence.
Soon you will hear the sounds
    of people changing their plans,
        dandruff falling,
        leaves changing color, and
        rainbows spanning the skies. (KFO)

Try to listen to the sound of clouds bumping
    or a car clearing its throat
    or grass growing
    or a leaf changing color.
Watch dragon clouds become fish
    or dancers or leaves or horses
    or something never before or never again
    and always changing. (KFS)

Listen to the sounds of grass growing;
listen to the sound of people changing their minds;
listen to the silence so that
    you'll better understand the words. (JTV)

I want to do something
   still and quiet.

I want to spend some
   time learning how
   plants talk to one another. (BHF)

A life-giving meal consists of dead beings;
personal solitude is necessary for community;
silence is the most potent language;
confusion is often the basis of creativity;
possessions tend to own the possessor. (KFL)

Instead of excessiveness,
I prefer incessiveness—
a single flower rather than a bouquet,
a solo instrument rather than a symphony,
a solitary popcorn kernel rather than a bagful,
a rock garden by moonlight,
a lingering glance. (KFR)

These are great mysteries I am grappling with—
    death
    madness,
    mysticism,
    androgyny,
    loneliness,
    hope,
    paradox.
These cannot be explained.
Mystery cannot be explained. (FFC)

I would like people to see
 death, failure, loneliness, confusion, and anger
 as not necessarily bad things,
 but as resources rather than enemies. (JBF)

There is always something about the song the wave sings to the shore that makes me stay by the seaside. Maybe it is the same wish that calls a moth to a flame or a leaf to the winds. There are times when I would like to gather the most powerful men in the world together on a beach and take them walking along the shore. They would go barefoot over the sand and I would ask them to make deep footprints and pretend that each step was a big business, a high office, an important award, a great victory, or a famous book. Then I would have them turn around and watch the waves erase their footprints. (KFS)

I know of an old man who studies sea life. He wakes up every morning before high tide and rushes to a certain spot on the ocean shore with his test tubes and bottles and carefully dips them into the water. Then he goes back to his home and thoughtfully looks at the sea life under his microscope. When the day is over he gathers his bottles and returns to the ocean—to the exact spot where he dipped them—and pours the little sea animals back to their home. Such a respect for the order and rhythms of the waters, and for the life it contains. (KFS)

I'm 70% water.
The world is 70% water,
and I think it's strange that
I've always lived on land. (BHF)

Several years ago I began formal preparations
　　for my death journey—
　　collecting maps, visas, consulate addresses,
　　vaccinations, traveler's cheques, other supplies.
There are still a few items missing,
　　but I feel basically ready.
There's no departure date,
　　and I haven't decided on my mode of transport,
　　but that will take care of itself I trust. (KFB)

In a sense
I believe in reincarnation.
My body will become reabsorbed in other elements—
raindrops, snowflakes, piss, a beer can—everything.
Mathematically there are six molecules of Buddha
in every square foot of air.
Sometimes I like to breathe in real deep
and try to get some Buddha in me. (BHF)

There is something wonderful about
seeing ordinary things in extraordinary ways.

Children see stones and think they're jewels.

It's all in the eye of the beholder—
        that sense of being a natural mystic
          of being recollected
          of being a saver of reality
     rather than simply a user of reality.
That's part of my concern as a fool.

That's part of my foolish wisdom. (FFC)

I'd like to be remembered as
    someone who delighted in paradox,
    who regarded both joy and pain as part of life.

I want to be remembered as
    someone who liked to simplify. (BHF)

Activities

Oh how I enjoy
eating a ripe persimmon
while deep, old bells boom!

Shiki
(KFF)

Mystical Water Fountain

This game may be played alone or with others. You will need for each participant a large glass filled with water and a comfortable place to sit. Take as long as you will to play this game.

1. Sit in the comfortable chair.

2. Take very small sip of the water. Notice something about the water as you swallow. Feel it within you. Feel the water's presence.

3. Repeat this procedure noticing a different thing about the water each time, until you finish one-third of the glass of water.

4. Repeat the same procedure as in number one, but this time notice something about yourself each time. Keep sipping and noticing until two-thirds of the glass is empty.

5. Now, spend some time with the remaining one-third glass of water. Notice its relationship to the glass. Notice, too, its relationship to you...and your relationship to the other "things" in the room. (RRH)

Plastic Burn

Get a piece of plastic, either a knotted clothes cleaner cover or a plastic six-pack holder (cut so that it stretches a double length). Suspend the plastic from a coat hanger over a large pan of water. Light the bottom of the plastic and watch it burn. Listen to the voice of the fire and the sound of the molten plastic as it strikes the water; see the fingers of smoke eddy upwards from the water and watch the strobe shadow of the spidery coat hanger on the ceiling. A vision of Pentecost! (KFC)

Inner-Outer

Go outside and look for a rock that expresses your inner self and a twig that expresses your outer self. Bring them back and share them in the community. Ritualize the collection of sticks and stones by burying, burning, exchanging or returning them to their original places. (KFC)

Cornstarch

Fill a bowl with a box of powdered cornstarch and add water, mixing the cornstarch in until all of the powder is first absorbed in the water; add no more water. Then strike the mixture smartly with your fist and observe that you cannot penetrate the solution. Place your finger gently in the mixture and it easily penetrates. Hold some cornstarch solution in your hands and shape it like a ball; it is malleable and seems to hold its shape until you release the pressure, whereupon it immediately liquefies in your hand. A mystery, a paradox, an object lesson in nonviolence! Add liquid food coloring to the solution and observe the evolving design which you can shape by the direction in which you turn the bowl. The eucharist of the counterculture! (KFC)

Rubber Cement

Gather a group of several people and coat your hands with rubber cement. Blow on them so that they begin to cool and dry, then join hands. As a fused community, move around and solve simple problems, like getting a drink of water, making a phone call. Each person has to be sensitive to the others' needs. Dance together, invite others to join your circle. Experience the fact that you are joined together by the sheer adhesion of your bodies as you freely swing your hands out. Then slowly separate yourselves from one another, a finger at a time (thumb, index, third, fourth, fifth) until you are joined by palms alone. Then slowly pull your palms apart and clap your hands. Carefully rub your hands together and watch the shower of little rubber cement balls. (KFC)

Forbidden Sounds

Form a circle of people with your eyes closed. Invite anyone to make a "forbidden sound," that is, one that expresses a thought, feeling, or experience about which that person might feel ashamed (heavy breathing), afraid (scream), or silly (babble). When someone makes a sound, everyone else must echo back the same sound twice. Then another person makes a different sound and hears it echoed. Since there are no words spoken and everyone's eyes are closed, privacy is assured and much healing can occur, especially when a forbidden sound is externalized and echoed. The effect is a mixture of confession, exorcism and group therapy. (KFO)

Neolith

Pretend that a chalk board is a cave wall and that the chalk is dinosaur blood. You are a gathering of cave people with no language, but you wish to share your experiences. Each participant is expected to draw a picture on the "wall" and then create a gesture and sound that express the picture. Everyone must imitate the respective tribal word-maker exactly: this is an oral tradition. Eventually a vocabulary of image/sound/gestures is developed and ideas can emerge by juxtaposing different "words" (water on top of fire means death of fire, water on top of flower means growth of flower). When the exercise ends, it is important to take time for "debriefing" to see how well the tribespeople remembered the original image/sound/gestures and what they understood by them (a picture of a blossoming flower might suggest alternately flower, springtime, growth, love or beauty to different people and its use would vary accordingly). (KFO)

The Manhattan Project

Foolish Brainstorming
for the Triennial Convention of the Episcopal Church
Andrew Foster, David Fly, Ken Feit, et. al. (March 1976)

1. Tug of War

Bring in rope and begin name calling to dramatize an issue; bring others into the struggle in the middle of the meeting. (Might use the same principle with pie-throwing or clown boxing match.)

2. Pin the Blame

Construct a board entitled "The Church" with various component parts (bishops, clergy, women, congregation, poor, blacks, gays, 1928 version of the Common Prayer Book, according to the issues of the conference). Then blindfold a participant and give him/her a dart or ribbon/paper labeled "blame" with a pin and after turning the person around several times have him/her throw dart or pin the blame on some faction of the Church. At the end of the day announce who or what issue was the most blameworthy.

3. Kool Aid

Set up a Kool Aid stand next to the hotel/convention bar at night. Offer free Kool Aid for anyone who will tell a story, sing a song, recite a poem, or do a dance. Wear clown white. It will make a powerful content/process with the slick bar where people are paying money (not offering an inside gift) to dull (not heighten) their senses. Variation: serve the Kool Aid in a segregated fashion having special cups for bishops, women, clergy or according to issues, for those who favor the traditional or revised Common Prayer Book. Eventually begin mixing the cups or the various kinds of Kool Aid to break down differences.

The Manhattan Project

4. Batter the Bishop

Bring several helmets appropriately marked "Bishop," "Ordained Woman," "Gay." Also have several baffle sticks, pillows, foam rubber lengths. Anyone can wear any helmet and contest anyone else for two minute bouts. Contestants can get out their inhibitions by swinging their weapons, shouting. Observers might wish to shout encouragement, boo. Participants will be required to shake hands before and afterwards. Variation: after the initial bout have the contestants exchange helmets and identities and continue the bout for two more minutes.

5. Rood Screen

Construct a large screen resembling a confessional. At certain times of the day allow anyone to go behind and make a speech or offer an explanation of "What I really meant to say," "What I really wanted to say," or "What I really should have said" on the convention floor. Observers will listen carefully and in all instances applaud and offer encouragement.

6. Process Language

By means of juggling or tight wire/plank walking dramatize the need for letting go (of a ball in order to receive the next one) and of balance in considering the issues of the day. Set up a plank/wire with catastrophe on either side (make extreme statements of each issue) and invite participants to walk across without falling. Teach conventioneers how to juggle.

7. Totem Pole

Using boxes, bags, masks (especially involving children perhaps in drawing them) create a totem pole of power/priorities at the convention. They shift or as new ones are generated, rearrange the pole (piling them on top of one another with a stick base). Announce who's on top of the totem pole and on the bottom for each day.

8. Graffiti Boards

Have sandwich boards (chalk boards or paper) with people walking around inside (walking graffiti boards). They can offer chalk or magic marker to anyone who cares to write down anything. Variations: Let the individual graffiti board be on a specific issue (I am Women's Ordination). After someone writes on the board, that person must wear it until someone else chooses to write. Collect the various (butcher paper) graffiti and paste them on walls around the conference to reflect the "grass roots" feelings. Install chalk boards or large paper pads in convention hall washroom stalls (along with chalk, pencils or magic markers). Let squatters write what they wish or conduct informal straw votes or key issues of the day. Announce the "stall returns" on each issue.

9. Punch and Judy

Have a Punch and Judy stage strapped to someone's waist and offer ongoing performances around the meeting area. Have Punch and Judy dramatize the issues of the conference in ribald fashion and answer questions from the onlookers. Variation: Have Mr. Punch or Ms. Judy offer awards each day to the speakers whom they favored and give their reasons.

The Manhattan Project

10. Monument
Build an ongoing sculpture (with Elmer's glue/plaster of Paris) from various conference items (paper, ash trays, beer cans, whatever anyone wants to donate). Let it reflect the process of the conference and the symbols that the conventioneers identify with.

11. Rat Race
Install a small racing platform with rats, turtles or symbolic movers each representing a segment of the convention or a specific issue. By shaking dice or urging on the racer, create a contest and announce the winner. Award a trophy at the end of the day.

12. Chess Game
Using standard chess pieces (renamed bishop, congregation, women) conduct ongoing chess games. At different times change the rules so that different movers have more/less power. Variation: create a giant chess board and conduct a festive game with viewers suggesting moves and with the movers themselves (humans) also deciding the issue.

13. Rituals
Using bamboo, rope, elastic and various kinds of background music (African, Near Eastern, Japanese, Russian, Israeli, American Indian) generate movements with shifting leadership. Using the tension of the rope dramatize the active/passive, in/out dynamics of situations (personal, national convention).

The Manhattan Project

14. Issue Popping
Carry "issue" balloons (with women's ordination, gay ordination, revised prayer book written on them). As the various issues are being debated, slowly blow up the respective balloon as well as its opposite). If one issue begins to wane, let air out of that balloon (raspberries) and begin again. Eventually when a vote is taken or the tide is turned, one of the balloons is popped. Use a microphone or bullhorn to emphasize the sound of escaping air from the deflating balloon. On one hand it will Bronx cheer the previous speaker (to the delight of the opposition); on the other hand the speaker will have the satisfaction of seeing the issue s/he opposes diminish. Everyone wins/loses.

15. Tension Breakers
When floor debate gets particularly heated, someone might arise with a point of order and ask everyone to look under their chairs for a piece of gum he put there earlier. Or else s/he might ask the floor for the solution to a crossword puzzle problem being worked out, especially if the answer touches upon the issues being debated.

16. Cleansing
Have people write or draw on a piece of paper what angers them or saddens them most about the convention. Collect the papers, merge them with Palm Sunday palms and burn them. Then anoint each other with the ashes. This might be followed by whiteface anointing.

17. The Answer Man

Have a Biblical type of person (long beard, flowing robes, self-confident) wander around the conference center accompanied by a disciple who is bearing a Bible. If anyone has a question of the Answer Man, he replies stentoriously with a Biblical reference which the disciple promptly reads in syrupy tones after which he righteously slams the good book shut and they both move on.

18. Fables/Stories/Puppets

Improvise appropriate stories, fables, proverbs, puppet dialogues for various issues, tensions in the conference. In some instances add inappropriate ones (let there be holes in your space, the earth is like a grain of sand only much heavier).

19. Communication Art

Adopt a different style of communicating for each day of the conference—one day in silence, another in a high pitched voice, or in slow drawl. Whenever anyone tries to remonstrate with you (come on, be reasonable, we're trying to do something serious here) reply in your voice and insist that you cannot understand them unless they use the same tone.

20. Church Activities

Take up a collection ad lib using standard collection plates and collecting whatever anyone will give; don't announce the cause. Come into the main room with towels and bowls of water. Begin washing the feet of the participants and drying them giving them towels to continue the process.

150

21. Kite Flying
Do things outside—in or out of make-up. Fly kites with issues/components of the conference written on them. Announce who flew the highest that day.

22. Carnival
Treating the whole convention as a carnival, create games, rides, freak shows.

> *Game:* a spinning wheel which determines the loser of the day or how convention funds will be allocated.
>
> *Ride*: Conduct a guided tour of the convention describing events in carnival metaphor.
>
> *Freak Show*: Exhibit caricatures of people, segments, issues in the conference. Wax eloquently on their freakiness, contradictions, uniqueness.
>
> *Medicine Show*: Sell an elixir which works wonders on the drinker (makes women acceptable as priests). Demonstrate the transformations in clownic fashion and sell bottles to onlookers.
>
> *Juke Box*: Invert cardboard television crate and install musician who will play or sing your favorite hymn or a portion of it (according to the amount of your donation).
>
> *Organ-Grinder/Monkey*: Do a clown routine with the organ grinder being the powerful one and the monkey the powerless one; then reverse their roles as issues/components within the conference.

The Manhattan Project

23. Beggar

Install a beggar/leper or otherwise "undesirable" who will simply panhandle people because he is hungry. On the last day the beggar will reveal himself/herself as a convention delegate who was exploring people's response to the issue of world hunger and announce his/her findings.

(The Manhattan Project from photocopied sheets)

Story-Listening with the Elderly

1. Help the storyteller feel comfortable. Ask where he or she wants to sit. Establish an informal conversational tone and chat for a while until you are both comfortable enough to start the interview, which might not even be during your first conversation.

2. Try using a tape recorder, if one is available, to provide permanent record of the conversation. This is less intrusive than note-taking, especially if the machine is kept below eye level, and it leaves you free to give the other person your complete attention. (If you are going to use the tape for any public purpose, you need to get a legal release signed by the other person.)

3. Be sensitive to whether the other person wants to be the center of a lot of attention or would be more comfortable if you kept the interview low-keyed. Many older people enjoy having several listeners and having their picture taken to record the event.

4. If the person is shy about talking about himself or herself at first, you might try discussing common interests. If you both like to hike, you might ask where other persons hiked when they were young, for instance, and what equipment they carried.

Story-Listening with the Elderly

5. Listen seriously. Give the other person your complete attention. Most people only hear each other with half an ear, if at all, no matter what their ages. Elderly people who repeat themselves endlessly often do so because they feel they are not really being listened to. Indicate your attention by asking thoughtful questions, picking up on significant points and gently guiding the elderly person from repetition. For instance, "Now that you've mentioned how awful it was when grandmother died, can you remember when you were first married?"

6. Tread carefully when you near sensitive issues. Do not pursue areas where you meet an unwillingness to talk. If older persons want to talk about something unpleasant, such as the death of a child, they will pursue it with little or no coaxing from you.

7. Be patient. Elderly people may tend to be wordy and to work their way through lengthy introductions. They are not part of today's test-wise, fill-in-the-blanks generation and may have a different style of talking. Sit back and hear them through if they are making a point in a roundabout way. Be guiding but non-bossy if the elderly person goes off on a tangent. "That's very interesting. Now could we get back to..." Be tuned into the difference between irrelevant side tracks and lengthy introductions.

Story-Listening with the Elderly

8. Have some questions in mind before you start, perhaps even a highly structured questionnaire.

9. Don't expect the elderly to use years for chronology. Use historical or personal points of reference for pegging questions. Ask what happened "right after the Depression," not what happened in 1940.

10. Allow them to express emotion. Oral history can be cathartic. Don't necessarily stop the interview because grandmother wants to wipe a tear away. But it's also better not to try to play amateur psychiatrist.

11. Be prepared for some blunt answers. As most people get older, they become less concerned with keeping up fronts of socially accepted behavior.

12. Ask questions about specific people to jog memories. Relatives are usually well remembered. Questions about brothers and sisters of the elderly person often lead to revelations about his or her own way of life of long ago.

13. If you are compiling a family genealogy, interview as many members of your family as possible.

Story-Listening with the Elderly

14. Accept that what elderly people tell you is not always fact and that two versions of events might conflict. The elderly are no more apt to lie or exaggerate than anyone else, perhaps less so, but memories are often only personal interpretations.

15. Do not interview people, including married people, jointly. Don't choose one member of a couple to interview over another. Ask which one wants to be interviewed, or interview them both—separately.

16. Avoid embarrassing memory failures if possible. If a person's memory is spotty, try asking easy questions that anyone who lived in that time or place would be able to answer. For instance: "Did they have horses and buggies then?" Not, "Do you remember the factory on Z Street?"

17. Gracefully accept gaps in the older person's memory. Don't press or embarrass them. If you really want to know the answer to a question, try coming back to that topic later, perhaps on another day. Many memory gaps are temporary.

Story-Listening with the Elderly

18. You can try to interview someone with a bad memory or even someone who is senile. Memory loss tends to progress from the present backward, with the oldest memories being among the last to fade.

19. Be non-judgmental. Listen to the other persons with regard for their point of view.

20. Remember that the elderly tire easily. Few can reminisce for more than 1 1/2 hours at a time. For many, half an hour may be the limit.

21. If you want to become the family historian or get seriously involved in oral history, consider further study, e.g., historical monographs of various ethnic groups, periods of migration.

(Story-Listening with the Elderly from photocopied sheets.)

African Storytelling

Characteristics of African storytelling:

1. Each character (e.g., animal) has its own voice/tone and movement (e.g., Momba, the ground hornbill, speaks in a deep rumbling voice, whereas Sulve, the hare, speaks with vivid piping accents—Lamba tribespeople).

2. Sometimes special sounds/words are attributed to certain animals. (There are standardized Hausa words for the sound of dogs quarreling and barking, wildcat's call, and crow of rooster—falsetto or nasal twang; among the Bushmen the sound "tt" is added to the first syllable of every word of the Blue Crane and the Tortoise's lisping makes him change all the clicks and other initial consonants into labials.)

3. The storyteller creates vivid effects by variations and exaggerations of speed, volume and tone (e.g, abrupt breaks, pregnant pauses, parentheses and rhetorical questions).

4. A form of onomatopoeia (ideophonic) is often used to add elegance and vividness to the narration. (e.g., "Tirin!"—Limba boy leaping into a lake; "Kado!"—Akan spider hitting the ceiling; "Kwata-kwata-kwata"—Luba chase; "Seki-Seki-Seki"—Mabale tortoise swimming; "Fu-Fu-Fu"—Mabale pheasant fluttering its wings; "Mek-Mek-Mek-Mek-Mek"—iguana crawling through a reedy waterhold; "Krik-Krik-Krik-Krik"—snake scurrying across a clearing; "Kaa-Kaa-Kaa"—a crow crying.)

African Storytelling

5. The audience is expected to make verbal contributions—spontaneous exclamations, actual questions, echoing of the speaker's words, emotional reaction to the development of the story, choral rejoinders, and ritual responses to the story—prologue and epilogue. (N.B. Singing is an element that is part of virtually all genres of storytelling, except probably specialized historical narratives.) Functions of singing: (a) helps to mark the structure of the story (e.g., ritual testing of hero); (b) adds musical aspect—extra dimension—for enjoyment and skill (e.g., drums or other musical accompaniment are sometimes story preludes); (c) provides a formalized means for audience participation.

6. Often the storyteller establishes personal virtuosity by special tricks of verbal style and presentation and interaction with the audience. (e.g., linguistic variations on a basic theme, individual treatment of various incidents, characters and motifs.) N.B. Actually there is no one correct version of a story. It is subject to infinite combinations and recombinations of motifs and episodes. New subject matter (topical) is frequently introduced in an effort to retain the interest of the audience. Purists who emphasize African storytelling as a static tradition of the folk/masses overlook the incredibly creative contribution of the individual.

7. Some storytellers actually move among their audience.

8. Others adorn themselves with paint, skins and/or masks and enact silent dreams. (e.g., southern Bushmen).

African Storytelling

9. In general storytelling is practiced by non-professionals (spare time skill, popular art).

10. Shifting regional variations determine who is most suitable for storytelling (e.g., older women among the Thunga, Ronga, Zulu, Xhosa, and Cameroons Fulani; men among the Limba, Hausa, Fang, and Pygmies; children among the Igbo, Dogon, and Galla).

11. Stories are generally told in the evening when the work is done or during the day when people have to spend long hours on drawn out but not very exacting tasks (herding, mending fish nets, guarding crops). A good time for storytelling is the Harmattan or dry season when there is no work or in the evening by full moon or campfire. (The Zulus have a saying, "Anyone who tells stories during the day will grow horns." The Kamba say that the cattle of anyone who tells daytime stories will give no milk or die.)

12. Sometimes stories are introduced with riddles and proverbs to gather the audience's interest.

13. Most of the stories carry a specific moral and serve a cautionary as well as an entertaining function.

14. During an evening of storytelling when the first person rises to leave, this proverb is usually spoken by the storyteller or some other member of the group, "It's only one man who spoils the entertainment of the night" (i.e., the first one to leave since others will soon follow). Sometimes this intimidates the person into staying. The

African Storytelling

Igbo sayings are "Anyone who leaves the pits without carrying any mud will suffer from a severe sickness," and "If you leave before the story is finished, yaws (illness) will prepare a soup (with poisonous mushrooms) for you."

Ritual Introductions to Stories

Fjort, West Equatorial Africa:
Narrator—"Let us tell another story; let us be off, let us be off."
Audience—"Pull away." (drummers prelude story)

Ewe, West Africa:
Narrator—"My story is of so-and-so."
Audience—"We hear" or "We take it up."

Hausa, Nigeria:
Narrator—"A story. A story. Let it go. Let it come." "See her (e.g., the spider) See her there."
Audience—"Let her come and let us hear."

Nilyamba, Central Africa:
Narrator—"A story. How does it go?"

Akan:
Narrator—"We do not really mean, we do not really mean (that what we are going to say is true)."

Mende, Sierra Leone:
Narrator—"Story or stories" (Domae or Domaesio)
Audience—"We're with you." (Ja Kundae)

African Storytelling

Igbo, Nigeria:
Narrator—"I have a story to tell you."
Audience—"Tell us."

Typical Story Beginnings
Limba:
"A woman once came out (on the earth)."
"A spider once got up and ..."
"A chief once married a wife ..."

Kamba:
"How did it happen?"

Kimbundu, Angola:
"I often tell of ..."

Luba:
"That which did—leopard and bushbuck (or other characters)."

Xhosa:
"It happened once long ago according to a story."

Ritual Closings to Stories
Kamba:
Narrator—"May you become rich in vermin in your provision shed, but I in cows in my cattle-kraal."
Narrator—"May your cattle eat earth and mud, but mine the good grass."

Bura, Nigeria:
Narrator—"Do not take my life, take the life of a crocodile (notorious for long life)."

African Storytelling

Swahili:
Narrator—"If this is good, its goodness belongs to us all and if this is bad, its badness belongs to that one alone who made this story."

Kimbundu, Angola:
Narrator—"I have told my little story, whether good or bad."

Hausa, Nigeria:
Narrator—"Off with the rat's head."
Narrator—"Here it is for you."

Akan:
Narrator—"This is my story, which I have related, if it be sweet, (or) if it be not sweet, take some elsewhere, and let some come back to me."

Mende, Sierra Leone:
Narrator—"That which I have seen I have told."
Narrator—"That which I have heard I have told."
Narrator—"My story points to you." (Narrator challenges a person to tell a story.)

Bini:
Narrator—"I am finished now, (pointing to another) it is your turn."
Audience—(clapping their hands) "Hear! Hear! Hear!" or "Well done! Well done!"

(African Storytelling from photocopied sheets.)

Children's Stories

(Told by Children)

Process:
Spend time with each child sitting on the floor and listening until you have gained the child's confidence. Then offer to *write down* (not tape record since the child must experience direct power over the story-listener) whatever story the child wishes to make up or tell *exactly* as it is told (not edited to correct gender, tense, number, mood) and to read it back to the child. The child can tell the story; the listener as scribe can read and write (which the child perhaps cannot do). It is the ancient relationship between pharaoh and scribe, emperor and chancellor, business executive and secretary—a merging of powers in the service of story. For the child it is magic to feel the submission of adult scribe, to see the unintelligible words on paper and know they came from his/her mouth.

At first the child may test you by abusing power—e.g., telling the story too quickly for you to write, using incessant repetitions or nonsense words to bedevil you, but be patient and write what you hear, asking for clarification when necessary. This will delight the child and merit your trust. Then usually the child will settle down to the rhythms of stories told carefully and caringly.

(The following are examples of stories told to Ken Feit in the above manner at a Montessori school in Milwaukee, Wisconsin, during the fall/winter of 1971–1972.)

Children's Stories

Once upon a time there was a haircut man and I came in and the haircut man cutted my hair all off and I hated it cause I like my hair long and lived happily ever after. (John, 5)

Once upon a time there was a daddy cat and a momma cat and a baby cat and they all ate some porridge and the momma cat said, "Too cold." And the baby cat said, "I don't like porridge." The father cat said, he said, "Too hot this porridge is." The baby cat said, "Can we catch a mouse?" The father cat said, "There isn't no mouse." That's the end. (Adam, 4)

Once upon a time there was a devil and there was a walking in the woods poop. Then a orange came and they made friends with that poop. And then the devil came and he took those two up and throw them down the toilet and flush them down the toilet. They came out the toilet. The top was opened and they came out and then the witch came and they lived happily ever after. (Randy, 6)

There was a smile with a light bulb on it and everybody thought he was funny and then a wicked witch came and turned him into a bell—ding dong and then he put it on Ken's glasses (hahahahahahahahaha). Then the bell turned into a nutty Richard. And then the good god-mother said, "Never look at the wicked witch so sleep a lotta times." And that's how we do the story of the Holy Time so then my mother said, "Do not never wake up in the sneeze." And then I woke up on a sneeze. "And never throw up on your nice, beautiful clothes and wear a pair of slippers under your beautiful clothes so you don't fall down and keep it quiet in my house." (Kathleen, 5)

Children's Stories

There is a boy and a girl's name Jack and Jill. And the boy came and Jack fall down and hurt his leg and Jill came and carried him home and give him some chocate and some banilla and a big giant named Mark and John came and stole all his food and his furniture. And he woke up and said, "Who stole my fish and my daughter's perfume?" And they lived happily ever after. (Amy, 4)

Once there was a little man and he told the doctor to fall downstairs and he bumped his head on the wall and then he falled down Adam's shirt and then he falled into his head and then he falled into his self and then he falled down on all the Ken's words that he wrote and that's the end-e-o. (Lonnie, 4)

Once upon a time there lived a old dragon. It was black and lived in a castle. He was happy cause he fires the tree. A wolf came and the dragon fired the wolf and eated him up happily ever after. (Chris, 5)

A witch came along and he want some sheep and make some furniture out of it and five men came along and five girls and saw the furniture. And they took it in a airplane and a rocket ship so they hurried to the house. The men sat down on the sheep and ran away and he got dead and...the boat had a lot of crocodiles and sheep and giraffes and buffaloes and sheep and bears. So a big witch came in the forest a little and the wicked witch took him home...wicked witch it rained outside in the rain and the ghost went into the motor and he got up and he just wanted his friend to come back. He almost come back someday he did come back. The wicket witch came along and so ten, ten, ten, ten, ten, ten, ten wolfes came and rah, rah, rah, crunch! Wicked witch got dead, dead, dead, wicket up so get out of bed and he died, how he died under garage and he cried. Buffalo stabbed him. Wicked witch only liked him. Happy New Year! (Johnny, 5)

Once upon a time there was an old, old woman with a father but they had no children, no children at all. And in the winter the wife said, "I think I'll go to take the children to the village today." While she was on the way to pick the children up she saw some snow on the ground. Then she started to make a snow girl. Then the old man came out. Then he started to help the old woman make a snow girl. Then the old woman and the old man said, "If only these children were real." "Well," the snow girl said, "Why, I am real." Then the mother and the father said, "Will you stay and be our snowchild?" Then they noticed that she only said half of the question. Then when it was springtime when the old woman looked out of her bed, they only saw a pile of water. And that's the end.
   (Cindy, 5)

Once upon a time the whole world was exploding with a terrible earthquake and it was storming out and it happened last night when we were asleep and there was a little monkey in our house and sleeped in our house last night and a spider and a splosion happened to be a terrible, terrible one. And the splosion was a terrible dragon and another nother nother dragon and a hundred hundred dragons and my brother was trying to kill the dragon, he was six years old and he had a gun with the father. The End. (Rebecca, 4)

Children's Stories

My centipede is called Beehunter and he has lots of hands to tickle me with; he has 22 hands. He lives under the house and eats dirt. He made his house himself and it isn't very good. His mother lives there too and her name is Sheema. (Desmond, 7)

Once upon a time there was a nice mother and father and they had two beautiful children, a boy and a girl and one night they invited their grandmother over and their grandfather. And that night it was Christmas eve and St. Nicholas was to come because they knew if they were good they would get nice presents from him. And it was a nice day, but on Sunday everybody was surprised. There was no stockings. There was no presents. And they went way up to the South-North Pole and talked to Santa about it because they were so good. "But mother and father and children, I ran out of toys and my elfs were dead and I am a very old Santa Claus. I'm only made to give the toys. And Mrs. Santa is only meant to make the cookies." And that's the end. (Cindy, 5)

Once upon a time there was a guy. He had a screw in his belly. And he went to this doctor and he said, "Can you please get this screw out of my belly?" Well, then the doctor told him to go to this museum, you know, and you turn left and you go straight and then you turn a left again and there's the museum. So he said, "Please can you get this screw out of my belly?" And then the museum guy, he told him to go into the desert and eat these green things, you know. And the storm came up and the screw unscrewed and his bottom fell off and his belly came off. And then the museum guy and the doctor lived happily ever after. (Adam, 5)

Children's Stories

Snowdrops are like little, little lights in a town at night time, only they would be in a very little, little town. Snowdrops are umbrella for flies. They could be dresses for spiders and things like that. (Mona, 7)

I had a horse; one day he died. I don't know where he died—he just died on himself. (Stuart, 5)

(Children's Stories from photocopied sheets.)

Bibliography

Works by Ken Feit

(Arranged in chronological order)

KFS   *Soundways: A Book of Sound Poems.* Chicago: Loyola University Press, 1971.

KFC   "Creative Ministry." *Celebration* (March, May, June, July 1974): insert.

KFL   "Laughter is a Sacrament." *One World* (January/February 1975): 9–10.

KFP   "The Priestly Fool." *Anglican Theological Review* (June 1975): 97–108.

KFH   "In Praise of Hands." *Liturgy* (January 1976): 6–18.

KFO   "Reflections of a Sound Poet." *Liturgy* (May 1976): 149–154.

KFM   Letter to Friends. (Chicago, 1980): trip to China.

KFJ   Letter to Friends. (Chicago, 1981): trip to Near East.

KFF   "The Cosmic Fool Haikus." *Bear & Co.: the little magazine* 5 (1981): 7.

KFB   "Letter to My Friends on the Occasion of my Fortieth Birthday." *Theaterwork Magazine* (July/August 1982): 24–31.

KFR   "Reflections of a Foolish Storyteller." *Theaterwork Magazine* (July/August 1982): 32–37.

Other Works Cited

(Arranged alphabetically by author)

JBF   Bailey, Jerome. "He's Not Foolin'." *Milwaukee Journal* 14 December 1976.

MBC   Ball, Millie. "Ken the Clown Cuts Up Paper." *Times-Picayune* (New Orleans) 18 July 1972.

WBP   Brueggemann, Walter. *The Prophetic Imagination*. Philadelphia: Fortress Press, 1978.

JCJ   Carpenter, Jolene. "From Jesuit to Jester..." *Grand Rapids Press* 4 August 1974.

JDS   Doody, Joan. "Jester Feit Skips to Campus." *The Lawrentian* (Lawrence University) 1 February 1974.

PFC   From a performance recorded in *Fools for Christ* (Cathedral Films) on 3 June 1978.

FFC   From an interview recorded 2 June 1978 by Jim Friederich during the filming of *Fools for Christ. Fools for Christ* (41 minutes) is available from Cathedral Films, P.O. Box 4029, Westlake Village, CA 91359. Video purchase: $39.95. 16mm rental: $48.00. To order by phone: 1–800–338–3456 (outside CA), 1–818–991–3290 (within CA).

MFE   Fox, Matt. "A Eulogy Re-Membering Ken Feit and other Cosmic Fools." *Bear & Co.: the little magazine* 5 (1981): 2–5.

MFW   Fox, Matthew. *Western Spirituality: Historical Roots, Ecumenical Routes*. Sante Fe: Bear & Co., 1981.

JFC   Friedrich, Jim. "Clown of Jesus." *Plumbline* (October 1981): 16–17.

BGR   Gilmour, Bob. "Religion and Clowns Have Much in Common." *Edmonton Journal* 29 March 1975.

GGC   Gurtner, George. "Church Smiles through Ken Feit." *Clarion Herald* (New Orleans) 12 July 1973.

BHF   Hayes, Bob. "Ken Feit: The Fool on the Hilltop." *The Hoya* (Georgetown University) 23 February 1973.

MHF   Hintz, Martin. "This Fool Isn't Joking." *Milwaukee Sentinel* 27 January 1973.

CHP   Hyers, Conrad. "Paper-Bag Mass." In *The Comic Vision and the Christian Faith*. New York: Pilgrim Press, 1981, pp. 82–84.

UBK   "Ken the Fool to Perform." *University of Baltimore Student Press* 10 December 1974.

JKF   Keys, Janice. "Fool Called Only Person of Truth." *Winnipeg Free Press* 5 June 1975.

JLR   LaRose, Joseph. "Young Jesuit Clowns Around." *Clarion Herald* (New Orleans) 13 April 1972.

PLF   Locher, Paul. "Professional Fool Delights Lowry Audience." *Daily Record* (Wooster, Ohio) 25 January 1975.

UWM   "Mime." Lecture and Fine Arts flyer. Wausau: University of Wisconsin, September 1975.

ROF   Oughtred, Russell. "Fool for Month Seeks to Show Wonder/Mystery of Life." *Lethbridge Herald* (Lethbridge, Alberta) 9 March 1975.

CAP   Port, Cathy A. "Itinerant Fool Is Rarely Bored." *Daily Camera* (Boulder) 16 October 1976.

DPF   Pyette, David. "Feit Celebrates the Fool." Montreal Star 21 October 1975.

RRH   Radley, Roger. "A Heart Line." *Bear & Co.: the little magazine* 5 (1981): 12–13.

JSP   Sale, Jonathan. "Fooling People all the Time." *The Guardian* (London) 30 December 1976.

TJS   Smith, Thomas J. "Peers at Christianity through Eyes of Clown." *Herald Citizen* (Milwaukee) 15 May 1971.

JTV   Toddie, Jean. "Fool Shares His Vision." *Elizabeth Daily Journal* (Elizabeth, New Jersey) 26 March 1977.

CTK   Tufford, Carolyn. " 'Fool' Poses Questions, Proposes No Answers." *Daily Herald Telegraph*, (Bloomington) 25 February 1977.

Other Works by Ken Feit

Letter to Friends. (Chicago, 1978): trip to India.

Letter to Friends. (Chicago, 1979): trip to West Africa.

"Storytelling." *Liturgy* (April 1973): 16–17.

"Storytelling." *Liturgy* (July 1976): 215–217

"Storytelling." *Liturgy* (August 1976): 249.

Feit, Ken and Matt Fox. "The Storyteller as Prophet." *Bear & Co.: the little magazine* 5 (1981): 6–7.

Other Works
(Arranged alphabetically by author)

Bliss, Shepherd. "Ken Feit: Presente." *Theaterwork Magazine* (July/August 1982): 40–41.

"Compassionate Clown Dead in Auto Crash." *National Catholic Reporter* 28 August 1981.

Larson, Roy. "A Fool for All Seasons." *Chicago Sun Times*: Midwest Magazine, 2 December 1973.

Leviton, Richard. "Clowning Around." *East West*
(August 1987): 58–63.

Liebenow, Mark. "Ken Feit." In *Is There Fun After Paul?*
San Jose: Resource Publications, Inc., 1987, p. 54.

Lorenz, Nan. "The Fool as Prophet." *Creation*
(March/April 1985): 24–25.

Martin, Joseph. "A Spiritual Shtick: Clowning with
Compassion." *Creation* (September/October 1985):
16–19.

——————— "My Clown as Spiritual Director."
Review for Religious (July/August 1987): 590–597.

——————— "Clowning as Liberation Theology."
Modern Liturgy (February 1989): 10–13.

Nisker, Wes. "Crazy Wisdom." *Yoga Journal*
(January/February 1989): 83ff.

Riemer, George. "How Many Provincials Have Their
Phones Bugged?" In *The New Jesuits*. Boston:
Little, Brown & Co., 1971, pp. 299–332.

"The Ritual Meal." (a photo essay) *Liturgy* (December
1975): 347–349.

Samra, Cal. "Fools for Christ's Sake." In *The Joyful
Christ*. San Francisco: Harper & Row, 1986,
pp. 39–51.

OTHER IMAGINATIVE RESOURCES FOR MINISTRY

FINDING THE CLOWN IN YOURSELF:
Personal Growth for Every Christian
by Jack Krall and Jan Kalberer
Paperbound, $8.95, 104 pages, 5 ½" X 8 ½"
ISBN 0-89390-179-2
Two active clowns show you how to get started in Christian clowning by first finding "the little clown" in yourself, and developing your own spirituality through your clown. Each chapter ends with a Scripture reflection, questions for self-examination, and suggestions for further reflection.

IS THERE FUN AFTER PAUL?
A Theology of Clowning
by R. Mark Liebenow
Paperbound, $9.95, 150 pages, 6" X 9"
ISBN 0-89390-066-4
Explore the history and foundations of laughter and clowning in the Christian Church. See how clowns can touch, heal, and nurture people, and survey the major types of clowning going on in the church today.

WORSHIP THROUGH THE SEASONS:
Ideas for Celebration
by Mary Isabelle Hock
Paperbound, $8.95, 106 pages, 5 ½" X 8 ½"
ISBN 0-89390-104-0
Worship planners: Make the assembly part of the action with help from these songs, dramatic sketches, pageants, movement scripts, and symbolic actions. Involves children and adults in any congregation.

NO KIDDING, GOD, WHERE ARE YOU?
Parables of Ordinary Experience
by Lou Ruoff
Paperbound, $7.95, 100 pages, 5 ½" X 8 ½"
ISBN 0-89390-141-5
Ruoff shows you where he finds God: in a bottle of whiteout, in a hand of poker, in a game of hopscotch. These 25 stories work most effectively as homilies; and to help you with your planning, they are accompanied by Lectionary references.

THREE-MINUTE DRAMAS FOR WORSHIP
by Karen Patitucci
Paperbound, $11.95, 260 pages, 5 ½" X 8 ½"
ISBN 0-89390-143-1
Here are 72 simple-to-do, easy-to-memorize, bible-based skits perfect for your church, classroom, or prayer group. Theme and Scripture reference at the beginning of each play will help you decide which ones best fit your particular needs.

THE GOLDEN LINK:
Gospel Playlets for Schools and
Parish Liturgies
by Larry Mullaly
Paperbound, $8.95, 128 pages, 5 ½" X 8 ½"
ISBN 0-89390-058-3
19 short plays, each one for a different Sunday liturgy during the church year. Structured for children from primary grades (five plays), middle grades (seven plays), and junior high grades (seven plays), they involve children but should be performed at adult Sunday liturgy.

HOW THE WORD BECAME FLESH
by Michael Moynahan, S.J.
Paperbound, $10.95, 135 pages, 6" X 9"
ISBN 0-89390-029-X
Bring Scripture to life with this collection of simple-to-use story dramas that embody the deepest gospel messages. Complete staging instructions make these easy to use in church with adults or in school with young adults.

WORSHIP DRAMAS FOR CHILDREN
AND ADULTS
by Cathy Lee and Chris Uhlmann
Paperbound, $11.95, 180 pages, 5 ½" X 8 ½"
ISBN 0-89390-130-X
These 38 simple dramatic ideas are designed for your use in creative worship, retreat, and prayer group settings. The performances are outlined step-by-step so that you can do them even if you've had no experience in the arts. Few props and no major memorization of lines are required.

COME MIME WITH ME:
A Guide to Preparing Scriptural Dramas for Children
by Gail Kelley and Carol Hershberger
Paperbound, $10.95, 90 pages, 8 ½" X 11"
ISBN 0-89390-089-3
A "can't miss" formula for presenting children's drama. The authors show you how to write your own dramas using a narration led by an adult with parts acted out by children. Includes 10 dramas.

ANGELS TO WISH BY:
A Book of Story-Prayers
by Joseph J. Juknialis
Paperbound, $7.95, 136 pages, 6" X 9"
ISBN 0-89390-051-6
This book is best suited for use in preparing liturgies and paraliturgical celebrations. Most of the stories are accompanied by scripture references, prayers, and activities.

THE MAGIC STONE
and Other Stories for the Faith Journey
by James L. Henderschedt
Paperbound, $7.95, 95 pages, 5 ½" X 8 ½"
ISBN 0-89390-116-4
Put the word of Scripture in context with today's lifestyles and the word becomes reality for you. Share them aloud and the word comes to life for your congregation, prayer group, or adult education class.

THE TOPSY-TURVY KINGDOM: More Stories for Your Faith Journey
by James Henderschedt
Paperbound, $7.95, 120 pages, 5 ½" X 8 ½", ISBN 0-89390-177-6
Henderschedt helps us to see ourselves in the characters he paints so vividly in his stories—perhaps as the bully Jason, in the title story, or as the two frail young people in "The Dance." There are a total of 21 imaginative stories in this book—all keyed to the Lectionary.

TELLING STORIES LIKE JESUS DID: Creative Parables for Teachers
by Christelle L. Estrada
Paperbound, $8.95, 92 pages, 5 ½" X 8 ½", ISBN 0-89390-097-4
Bring home the heart of Jesus' message by personalizing his parables. Each chapter includes introductory comments and questions, an easy-to-use storyline, and discussion questions for primary, secondary, and junior high grades.

Ask for these books at your local dealer, or complete the order form below and send it to

Qty	Title	Price	Total
___	_____	____	____
___	_____	____	____
___	_____	____	____
___	_____	____	____
___	_____	____	____
___	_____	____	____
___	_____	____	____
___	_____	____	____
___	_____	____	____
___	_____	____	____

Subtotal _____

California residents add
6% sales tax _____

*Postage & Handling _____

Total amount enclosed _____

Resource Publications, Inc.
160 E. Virginia Street, Suite 290
San Jose, CA 95112-5848.

(408) 286-8505

*Postage & Handling
$1.50 for orders under $10.00
$2.00 for orders of $10.00-$25.00
9% (max. $7.00) of order for orders over $25.00

☐ My check or money order is enclosed.

☐ Charge my ☐Visa ☐MC Exp. date: _____

Card No. _____-_____-_____-_____

Signature: _____

Name: _____

Institution: _____

Street: _____

City: _____ State ____ Zip _____

Code: FW